Praise

The Soulful Journey of Recovery

"Of the many books on trauma, codependency, and children of alcoholics, *The Soulful Journey of Recovery* stands out as a groundbreaking work. Tian Dayton has synthesized current research, behavioral theory, and her years of experience in creating a must-read not just for those that have grown up in families of trauma but for clinicians who work with these individuals. Her understanding of what happens to a child physically, emotionally, and spiritually and how these experiences manifest in adult relationships is astounding. Dr. Dayton has a true gift for writing with clarity and inspiration and this book is no exception. *The Soulful Journey of Recovery* goes far beyond our notions of codependency and trauma-related issues and provides the reader with a deeper understanding and practical tools that will assist in healing."

—**Rokelle Lerner,** Senior Clinical Advisor of Crossroads Antigua;
author of *Daily Affirmations for the Inner Child, Daily Affirmations for Adult Children of Alcoholics,* and *The Object of My Affection is in My Reflection;*
founding member of the National Association for Children of Addiction

"Once again, as a great author, Dr. Tian Dayton has brought forth words that touch our hearts and souls. There are millions of us who were confused, devastated, and in emotional pain because of the addiction and the havoc that addiction played in our lives. She has reached in and pulled out the deep strength and courage that each of us houses inside our often 'too busy' minds, aching hearts, and tired bodies. For the time we read her book, *The Soulful Journey of Recovery,* we breathe deep, we relax our personal selves, and are able to recharge, understand, and feel our own inner gifts. This is a book that must be read once, put into our memory and action bank, and then read as often as we need to recharge. I enjoyed being able to it pick up and put it down, absorbing the wisdom of each chapter. Dr. Tian Dayton has produced another masterpiece, and I highly recommend this book to all of us who have held hands as we walked the journey of recovery from all addictions."

—**Sharon Wegscheider-Cruse,** author of *Learning to Love Yourself, Choicemaking, Another Chance,* and *Caregiving;* family therapist;
cofounder of the National Association for Children of Addiction;
founder of ONSITE Workshops, TN

"I have always loved Tian Dayton's work, and one more time, her words speak directly to me in my personal and professional journey. Whether you are new to her work or are a sage admirer, you will find yourself captivated, inspired, and furthered in your recovery journey. She has a great mastery of words as she cuts to the core and speaks the truth of those who have lived with trauma. As said in the introduction, recovery is not stopping something as much as it is beginning..."

—**Claudia Black, PhD,** Senior Fellow of The Meadows;
Director of the Claudia Black Young Adult Center;
author of *It Will Never Happen to Me* and *Unspoken Legacy;*
founding member of the National Association
for Children of Addiction

"*The Soulful Journey of Recovery* is a book that possesses the rare opportunity to simultaneously teach and emotionally touch the reader. Those children of all ages who have experienced trauma in their lives have the opportunity to read and reflect on the wisdom of Dr. Dayton. Her clinical expertise is obvious throughout the book. She is a master at helping others and is truly at the top of her game. This book will take the reader from personal traumas to shared recovery. I highly recommend her book to all who search for a journey to recovery. You will not be disappointed."

—**Robert J. Ackerman, PhD,** professor emeritus from
Indiana University of Pennsylvania; former Director of the
Mid-Atlantic Addiction Research and Training Institute,
author of *Perfect Daughters* and *Silent Sons;* cofounder of
the National Association for Children of Addiction

THE
Soulful
Journey OF
Recovery

A Guide to Healing from a Traumatic Past for ACAs, Codependents, or Those with Adverse Childhood Experiences

Tian Dayton, PhD

Health Communications, Inc.
Boca Raton, Florida

www.hcibooks.com

**Library of Congress Cataloging-in-Publication Data
is available through the Library of Congress**

© 2019 Tian Dayton, PhD

ISBN-13: 978-07573-2200-6 (Paperback)
ISBN-10: 07573-2200-X (Paperback)
ISBN-13: 978-07573-2201-3 (ePub)
ISBN-10: 07573-2201-8 (ePub)

All rights reserved. Printed in the United States of America. No part of this publication may be reproduced, stored in a retrieval system, or transmitted in any form or by any means, electronic, mechanical, photocopying, recording, or otherwise, without the written permission of the publisher.

HCI, its logos, and marks are trademarks of Health Communications, Inc.

Publisher: Health Communications, Inc.
        1700 NW 2nd Avenue
        Boca Raton, FL 33432-1653

Cover design by Larissa Hise Henoch
Interior design and formatting by Lawna Patterson Oldfield

To my husband Brandt N. Dayton.
With love and endless devotion.
Here's to a lifelong friendship, *friend*.

"Addiction rips through so many families and mine is no exception. In 2011, I lost my brother Hal to this disease. He was an addict and an alcoholic. He was also one of my favorite people on this planet. He was incredibly charming and quick witted, kind and generous, smart and quick to laugh. I miss him every day.

"My idea of recovery was limited because I associated sobriety with stopping. You know, you get sober . . . you stop drinking, stop doing drugs . . . you just stop. But my time on *Mom* has taught me that recovery is actually about starting. Starting to live a life that's bigger than you thought possible— where you can trust people and they can trust you, where you can heal relationships and let go of the past, where there's no problem that you have to face alone.

"On *Mom,* I get to see characters who were broken and defeated by alcoholism become part of a community filled with support, acceptance and unconditional love—and as a result of that, completely turn their lives around."

—Allison Janney
Excerpted from an acceptance speech for
Freedom Institute Mona Mansell Award

CONTENTS

FOREWORD

I was excited when my dear friend, author Tian Dayton, asked me to write this foreword. Immediately, my memory returned to the early 80s when, quite by chance, I met Janet Woititz who handed me her dissertation, *Adult Children of Alcoholics: Common Characteristics.*

ACoA landed atop the *New York Times* bestsellers list and signified the beginning of a significant grassroots movement that made an enormous contribution to our understanding of addiction as a disease that affects the whole family.

Dr. Dayton wrote the *The ACoA Trauma Syndrome* in 2012, expanding that body of knowledge and deepening our understanding of the family of origin that surround addiction, making its treatment relevant once again.

The ACoA Trauma Syndrome made the connection between the adult child of alcoholics syndrome (ACoA, also known as ACA) and post-traumatic stress disorder (PTSD) often experienced by children who grew up in addicted families long after they have left their families of origin. Tian answered their haunting question: "Why am I feeling the pain from my childhood now, as an adult, when I am no longer even living at home?"

The Soulful Journey of Recovery is more than a book. It is an invitation to journey along the continuous path of discovery, a pathway to healing the wounds of a traumatic childhood.

All of us who have been touched, directly or indirectly, by chemical or behavioral addictions and related mental health disorders can benefit from this continuing journey of self-awareness and recovery.

The Soulful Journey of Recovery responds to a need we're witnessing increase by the day, not only because of the opioid crisis but also the adverse childhood experience (ACE) movement that has opened the floodgates for millions who experienced the kind of relational trauma in childhood that is impacting their physical and/or mental health as adults.

The Soulful Journey of Recovery takes readers on an actual journey that ignites creativity and ingenuity. It jumps off the page and into the world of recovery. It asks the reader to dive in, to make a connection with life, to put an oar in the water and row. It's both an information and a practical "how-to" book, one that is sure to become a "go-to" for anyone in recovery from addiction, codependency, or adult children who had adverse childhood experiences and ACA issues.

Having spent the majority of my professional life creating platforms for some of the major voices of self-help and recovery, I know just how freeing, joyful, and life-altering this odyssey can be. In my own journey of recovery, I have found expressive/experiential therapies that get to the heart of the matter to be most effective to heal from childhood trauma.

The new generation of readers prefers multimedia and multisensory experiences to simply reading, and Tian, a former Montessori teacher and a master of psychodrama, has been a proponent of experiential learning her entire professional life.

We are in the midst of another movement whose time has come, one that has been brought into a new level of intelligence and understanding through the research on neuro-science, attachment and adverse childhood experiences.

Take this journey with Dr. Dayton—it promises to change your life.

—*Gary Seidler*
co-founder, Health Communications, Inc.,
and US Journal of Drug & Alcohol Dependence

ACKNOWLEDGMENTS

I would first like to acknowledge YOU, the reader, on your journey of recovery from childhood, relational trauma. You/we have carried a silent and difficult-to-see burden as children who grew up with parental addiction and the forms of abuse that invariably cluster around it. I acknowledge you for having the personal integrity and love for your children and grandchildren to identify and work through the issues created by living with addiction so that you can move into freer and more conscious lives and relationships. And so that you change the script for and alongside your families as best you can. In this way, you change the world and make it a better place.

Next, I would like to acknowledge the National Association for Children of Addiction (NACoA, nacoa.org) whose mission it has been to give a voice to the too often forgotten children trapped in a world of parental addiction and dysfunction, and NACoA's tireless and devoted CEO, Sis Wenger. NACoA is the oldest advocacy organization in the United States focusing on children of addiction, pleading their case because they are little and cannot advocate for themselves. It has been this organization's mission to speak for these children on Capitol Hill and to support the kind of legislation that will help them to get a better start. NACoA's strategy has been through creating quiet partnerships with Public Broadcasting Service (PBS) children's programming, Substance Abuse and Mental Health Services Administration (SAMSHA) programming, clergy, doctors, nurses and teachers alongside other forms of public advocacy, through all those, in other words, who touch the lives of children. NACoA has again and again left their own name out of their many accomplishments on behalf of these children in favor of getting the job of educating and advocating for them done. I would like to acknowledge their devotion to this cause and their effectiveness as an organization. Additionally, through the board members of NACoA who are leading experts in their respective fields donating their time, that work has been consistently professional and cutting edge. (See *nacoa.org/about-us/our-board/*).

I would also like to thank Christine Belleris, senior editor at Health Communications, for her help in bringing this book to print. Christine is always a joy to work with and to bounce ideas off of, her understanding of HCIs work is impressive. And a big "thank you" to Larissa Henoch for her thoughtful and creative help in making the graphics, and to Lawna Oldfield for preparing the charts, journaling pages, and laying out the manuscript so professionally. This is a great team to work with.

INTRODUCTION

The warrior's approach is to *say* "yes" to life:
say "yea" to it all. Participate joyfully in the sorrows of the world.
We cannot cure the world of sorrows, but we can choose to
live in joy. When we talk about settling the world's problems,
we're barking up the wrong tree. The world is *not* perfect.
It's a mess. It has always been a mess. We are not going to change it.
Our job is to straighten out our own lives.

—Joseph Campbell
A Joseph Campbell Companion:
Reflections on the Art of Living

Recovery kicks open a door in your soul. It is a moment of awakening. It takes you on a journey that changes everything. Recovery from growing up with addiction, adverse childhood experiences, or codependency is about becoming emotionally sober. It's coming into an awareness that there is something inside of you that is holding you back, interfering with your relationships, or creating unnecessary discord in your life. Doing something active to change that, to make things better, is recovery.

One of the gifts of recovery is being able to live in the present because you're not constantly getting triggered into feelings that belong to the past. It's being able to identify, manage, and express your feelings and then listen as someone else does the same. It's caring about yourself and about other people and not confusing taking care of yourself with isolating or pushing others away. It's letting go of the idea that your past could have been any different and proceeding with a reframing of the events of your life so that they sit differently inside of *you*. It's taking responsibility for yourself and where you are now in your life. Recovery is reclaiming your own joy and saying *yes* instead of *no* to life and love.

Addiction goes hand in hand with trauma. It is often the result of trauma and it causes more trauma. Wherever you fall on that spectrum, this book is written for you. If you're a child of an alcoholic you may feel like you are leafing through the pages of your own journal, like I have been reading your mail. If you're an addict in recovery, trauma work is important in preventing relapse and making sure that recovery doesn't only mean physical sobriety but emotional sobriety as well. If you're a child of adverse childhood experiences, which may include all that we've just discussed, you will develop an understanding of the forces in your life that undermined your health and what you need to do to improve that, and if you're a codependent, you may find out how you got to be one.

Being an adult child of an alcoholic (ACA) or growing up with adverse childhood experiences (ACEs) is like inhaling secondhand smoke. Someone else puffs away but your lungs get black. And the more you're in their orbit, the bigger the impact. Then the illness that was inside of them is now inside of you. Lots of us don't want to attend to such an illness because we're too mad about how we got it. We resent the work we have to do to get better from something that someone else caused. We spent our childhoods trying to help, picking up dropped balls and filling in the gaps left by our parents, being good kids who tried not to need too much—and now we have something wrong with us that *we* need to get help for? Seriously?

Or perhaps we have spent a lifetime seeing the problem as "out there," in another person, seeing ourselves as the victim of someone else's malady, so we have trouble seeing ourselves as someone who needs help or may be passing our unresolved and hidden pain and anger onto the next generation. But just because we don't see it, doesn't mean it isn't there. Because of the way we defended against knowing the kind of hurt we were experiencing as kids, because we shut down, adult children can carry pain, shame and anger without knowing it. The defenses that ACAs erect and perfect to *not feel* the pain of living around active addiction, to blot out the effects of various types of abuse, to rewrite or bend reality to make it somehow more palatable, mean that we can live in a kind of emotional ignorance. We simply *don't know that we don't know.*

As adult children we're great at thinking but not always so good at feeling. We try to think of ourselves as better because we don't want to do the sometimes painful emotional work that asks us to look into ourselves and try to understand why we do what we do. We want to avoid feeling those vulnerable, trapped and hurt emotions from our childhood that we think we've forgotten. But out of sight is not out of mind. Those unprocessed emotions can lay wait in our unconscious where they become the pain pump that fuels acting out behavior, physical illness and relationship issues. But when we can go within and make friends with some of that hurt, it is liberating. And it's efficient, it can take only a short time to come in touch with and process what we've spent a lifetime avoiding. And we can begin to walk a different path in which we can build on a better foundation.

Addiction is not a legacy that turns itself around by itself. Remember the whole point of using drugs and alcohol is to go unconscious, to medicate what we feel, to obliterate or deaden pain in our inner world. And that unconsciousness isn't limited to the addict alone. Everyone around the addict who has covered for them, denied that anything is amiss or simply hopped on board and in some way joined them is unconscious, too. And the same is true for other forms of abuse and neglect. But you don't have to stay stuck. You don't have to live with and live out the effects of someone else's disease. You don't have to make it your disease. You don't have to pass pain down to another generation. *You* can change, *you* can turn the legacy around and pass down health rather than dysfunction to the next two generations that you are impacting directly and those afterwards.

Amazingly it can take only a short time to come in touch with and process what we've spent a lifetime avoiding. We avoid it because we fear it, but feeling it is liberating and we develop a sense of inner confidence and mastery that we can take into all areas of our lives.

It takes work, time, dedication and a willingness to become aware. But the bonuses, the gifts are right there, built in. Because in becoming aware you transform your life. You become one of those people who are just sort of special, you start to live consciously rather than unconsciously. You come to value yourself, others and life. You trade a deathstyle for a lifestyle.

Learning is never meaningful until we make it our own and recovery is no different. That's why I have written this book as a path of self-discovery. Telling our own story is our right and privilege and it brings us in touch with our own creativity, it's a soulful journey.

I love the addiction field's tradition of giving all of the information needed to get better to the client and then providing a healing container through which to process emotions. I have done exactly that in *The Soulful Journey of Recovery*. Each chapter provides the theoretical information that any intelligent person will want to understand, in order to buy into the process of recovery. I have organized the book in the progression of information that you will need to know for a basic primer in the theoretical underpinnings of the recovery process and the flow of healing that I generally see clients pass through.

I have laid out the early chapters to give you the lay of the land, all of the information that will allow you to take hold of your own process.

Following many of the chapters, I have given you self-tests and processes that will allow you to assess for yourself which issues you identify with or need to work on. About two thirds of the way through the book we plunge more deeply into the healing process.

So this is a book about doing, about embracing the basics of recovery. It's about crafting the kinds of strategies that will make life changes sustainable and renewable.

If you already know a lot about recovery, it will deepen your understanding of the neuroscience of attachment and trauma and provide the kinds of exercises that will help you to become more of you. If you're just beginning to learn, it will help you to get going.

I have included an exercise after each chapter designed to help you to bring focus, clarity, and direction to what's going on inside of you, to get closer to your inner world. I have also created web pages (*tian dayton.com/soulfuljourney*) with video clips, guided imageries, and all sorts of recovery supports to enhance your healing experience.

Wherever you are now, know that there have been others who have been there, too. If you seriously and sincerely embrace the soulful journey of recovery, you will come to know a kind of peace, inner confidence, and happiness that will give you new ground to stand on. You will change your own life and the lives of those close to you. You will change the legacy of addiction and adverse childhood experiences from harm to hope and healing.

CHAPTER ONE

Coming Home: Understanding Relational Trauma

The truth is like a lion. You don't have to defend it.
Let it loose. It will defend itself.

—Max Plank

"Happy families are all alike; every unhappy family is unhappy in its own way." As arresting as I find Tolstoy's famous opening sentence from *Anna Karenina*, I disagree on this one point. Addicted families, I have found, are actually very much alike—unhappy in some very quantifiable and predictable ways. This was one of the first epiphanies of my recovery. It came from sitting in room after room of ACA, Al-Anon and CODA meetings, listening to and sharing our stories, feeling as if I could finish their sentences and they could finish mine. It seemed that somehow, in some mysterious way, we all grew up in the same living room, at the same kitchen table...in the backseat of the same car.

When people identified with something I shared at a meeting, I was dumbfounded. I thought, *Seriously, you're actually coming up to me to talk more and not telling me to leave?* For so many years, I had hidden the impact of this family illness, even from myself, beneath a veil of confusion and "loyalty." Now it seemed I wasn't alone after all. There were roomfuls of us, at least.

Because I could talk about my father's addiction, I thought I was open. But until I found recovery, I couldn't feel anything about it, I didn't really understand how it had impacted me, or for that matter, my family. I couldn't expose those places inside of me that were numb and unconscious, that made me feel little and vulnerable and put those inner experiences into words. I barely let myself know how alone and hurt I felt by growing up in this strange world of parental addiction and all of the mess that came with it. Now there appeared to be a way out of this perplexing muddle, this false complacency and damage.

And it was called recovery.

If you have picked up this book, you are probably already on your road to healing and recovery. You are already listening to that voice inside of you that says that you want more out of your life.—More peace, more understanding, more success, and better relationships. Perhaps you're well down the road and devouring materials and work-shops, have found a therapist and tried twelve-step meetings. Or, maybe you're just putting your toe in the water and simply want to get a sense of what's out there in terms of resources and what's in you that wants to reach out to them. Wherever you are, know that others have been there, too. You are not alone, you are in good company.

Whether you are an ACA (previously known as ACoA), an addict, or a child who grew up with the relational trauma of adverse childhood experiences, this book is written for you.

If you travel this path sincerely and in a reasonably organized way (nobody's perfect), you will gain enough clarity so that your past no longer runs you. And you will see life in a more appreciative and com-passionate way. You may always carry some emotional effects of trauma, but you won't care so much, because the wisdom and depth you will gain from facing and working through them will far outweigh the shortfalls. You will turn what could be a dark legacy into one of meaning and purpose. You will transform it through the alchemy of recovery.

I am writing this book because I grew up with addiction, and so did my husband. Together we have been boggled by the very complicated relational dynamics that growing up in this atmosphere creates. And let me be clear: when I say "addiction," I am also including what inevitably accumulates around it: neglect, abuse of all stripes and colors, despair. Addiction and relational trauma create some sort of "G force" that intensifies everything in it's surroundings. They're a magnet for dysfunction. Conflicts are hotter. Closeness is claustrophobic. Even the humor intensifies. Some of my best laughs are about the craziness that surrounds this disease. Belly laughs, where tears of recognition spring to your eyes, and you feel both exposed and vindicated, like a trap door flew open, and you could see into another world. Living with addiction can really help you sharpen your graveyard wit.

Let me try to paint a picture of what it is like to grow up with a parent who is an active alcoholic or is using drugs. First of all, I'd say that the picture is not easy to draw because it is constantly changing, shifting all over the map. It alternates between two very diverging worlds, a sober world and a drunk or high world, and each one has its own patterns. Each world has its own house rules. And in each world, the nature of the relationships, who is close to whom or distant and what is expected, needed, allowed, longed for, avoided, rewarded, or punished, can be radically different.

In world number one, let's call it, before addiction has permeated every corner, we may well be looking at a successful, even a special-seeming family. A family that looks good and has self-esteem. We might find cheerleaders, athletes, thespians, artists, and academic achievers. We'll see parents who appear to love each other and their kids. They have friends, and they go to church or synagogue or mosque. These are families who laugh, have fun, take vacations together, and generally seem to have a good life.

And then there is the "other" family, where addiction is more progressed and invasive. This is the family who is losing its footing, whose self-esteem is not so good anymore, who is insecure, questioning itself at every turn. In that family, things can be slowly or quickly coming apart. Some members work vigilantly to achieve and maintain the family self-worth, while others succumb to defeat and dashed hopes. Or, they withdraw or act out. And no one really knows quite what's happening because for every mortifying and scary "truth" that shows itself, the family tells themselves an "untruth" to lessen the pain. The family slips into denial and obfuscation. They go increasingly into *survival* mode. Like a boat that is slowly taking on water, they rotate watches, frantically bailing out in order to stay afloat, to keep from sinking further and farther down into a dark abyss.

Like Alice in Wonderland, trapped in a room that is constantly changing shapes, the child with an addict for a parent is constantly reaching for the walls, only to find the walls have become the ceiling, and the ceiling is now the door. Sometimes you feel very, very big, or very, very small. But you just can't quite land safely or find *normal* in that fluid and fluctuating world. You slide right by *normal*, or it slides right by you.

My own father was kind, attentive and responsible when he was sober and frightening and revolting when he was drunk. When he had enough scotch in him, my beloved dad became like something otherworldly, like in a movie, one of those characters who had pointed ears, who hopped, leaped, and even flew around the room. He became something ridiculous, terrifying, insidious, and strangely fascinating, something that found his way up to earth level, to my room, from a dark underworld. But *it* wore my father's face. *It* knew my name. Then, through no action of mine (I have come to realize), there he'd be again.

He would sober up and be my best friend and dad, the father who knew if I had a speech to write or a paper due, the one who understood me from the inside out and knew just what I liked for breakfast.

I am trying to paint a picture of the world of children who have to somehow become "used to" watching their parent cycle between being dead drunk and abusive and then, the next morning, return to life, thinking that nothing really bad happened because that drug and the alcohol wiped the addict's memory away. And when that addict sobers up in the morning and comes to breakfast with no recollection of the cruel and crazy person they were the night before, they want their family to join them in that delusion. And guess what? The family does. And this is what makes the family so sick and twisted up inside. And traumatized. This witnessing our parent careen between worlds, like some winged beast who forgot where home was, is deeply distressing for children, adolescents, and teenagers alike; it shakes our world order and messes with our insides. Because these drunks and drug addicts aren't living somewhere in outer space or even on the streets; they are the dads and moms we come home to after school. The mom we still make ourselves kiss goodnight as we choke back the urge to throw up at the stale smell of gin or the dad whose lascivious glare from days before flashes across our minds when he gives us a hug good night.

And then there is the functional drunk, the dad who holds down a steady job or the mom who takes pills and drinks "a little." And there is a lag time in the way she talks and moves around. She is the mom who does the basics, but also just spends a lot of time in her room with the door shut. We can't quite find her. And she can't quite find herself, but she is very, very busy—too busy for us. These are parents who bend our sense of normal just enough, so we go through life feeling like we're seeing double.

Recently I was at a wedding and my dinner partner, I quickly learned, was an ACA. We are everywhere it turns out. He said something so beautifully that I asked him if I could quote him.

My dad was a madman, you know, like the show, an advertising guy in the '50s. That's just the life he led; he worked hard. He'd get on the train every morning at 7:00 AM. He'd go to Madison Avenue…work all day in that environment, the whole thing, you know…the "boozy lunches"…all of it, then he'd be back for drinks and dinner at 7:00. Always like that."

He leaned back in his chair and tilted his head as if seeing something far away in the distance.

I remember it; I can just see it. I'd be sitting there and just exactly about halfway through dinner…I'd watch him turn into a different guy…right there in front of my eyes. And it went on just like that…every night.

This goes straight to the dilemma of the ACA. Because as kids we are forced to somehow find a way to integrate both dads and moms. We try to make one whole parent out of the person who is terrifying, hurting, or confusing us and the person who is taking care of us and loving us. And this wreaks havoc with our inner world; it makes us sick inside. But because it hurts so much and is so perplexing, and makes it hard to live our lives, we try not to feel it. We get up in the morning and go through the day trying not to think about what happened the night before. We defend against knowing some of the most impactful elements of our own personal experience, some of which shaped us. And because it happens every day, it becomes sort of normal.

When your parent is an addict, you lose something almost indescribable, you can't say things like, "See you soon" or "I will miss you." After my parents divorced—even though I was profoundly relieved that my dad was no longer drunk and in the basement, that I didn't have to run at the sound of his footsteps or fear his rage or insults or drunkenness—I still missed him. He was my father, the man who had raised me, provided for me, laughed at my little jokes, and admired my accomplishments. The father who loved me and who I looked up to. So we could not just say, "Bye, Sweetie, I will miss you," to reassure each other until we returned to a comfortable connection again, because the truth was we *never* returned, and we knew we probably never would. We did our best, we connected when we could. We returned as much as possible to that happy and comfortable father–daughter connection. But I knew in the back of my mind, and he in his, that these would always be stolen moments, there to remind us of what we once were, before alcohol changed everything. And to make matters even more difficult, my mother was a professional at sounding recovered *while* in denial. For her generation I think she did very well at facing my father's addiction and herself embracing Al-Anon. But the truth was, she always thought it was Dad who was the problem and she could never look at what she brought to the party and kept bringing to the party so really, we had two parents who were short circuiting.

It is an important developmental task for all children that we integrate the sides of our parent that we love with the sides we hate. It's part of growing up and moving into maturity, of accepting both the good and the bad and being able to see and live with both. But for the child living in addiction's blast radius, this becomes an Herculean task. We have so long defended *against* seeing the most frightening sides of our addicted/abusive parent and those sides scared and repulsed us so much that we can't just say, "Well, that's Dad," or "You know Mom." We tried so hard *not to know* those sides of them. And we may have idealized their better sides just to have something to hang onto, to get us through until the good parent showed up again or to hold onto once they were gone forever. Because these sides are so divergent, the bad sides remain split out of awareness, and the good sides stay idealized. And this kind of defended, rigid thinking can get projected onto the other parent as well. It's all or nothing, black and white, no shades of gray—dis-regulated. Then when we enter our own adult intimate relationships as partners and parents, we're still waiting for the bad side to show up, and we can't quite trust the good side.

CHAPTER TWO

Drunk: Trapped
in "Crazy"

It's often said that a traumatic experience early in life
marks a person forever, pulls her out of line,
saying, "Stay there. Don't move."

—Jeffrey Eugenides, *Middlesex*

I was a guest expert on MSNBC, commenting on actor David Hassel-hoff's strange video of himself on drugs. When his daughter tried to tell David how scary he was when he was high, he said, "Film me." This was, in my opinion, every ACA's dream—that their parent would actually give them permission to document themselves while drunk or high and then be willing to look at that film when they sobered up. That Dr. Jekyll and Mr. Hyde would be caught on tape. That there would be evidence.

Every ACA lives with these two different parents. Every ACA is forced to somehow reconcile a normal world with a world turned on its head by drugs and alcohol. In this case, that drunken parent was recorded so that healing and understanding could happen. David's willingness to be captured on video could verify the reality that generally gets denied and perhaps free his daughter from haunting scenes and memories that she might otherwise be told didn't really happen. Usually, this drunken side of the parent remains hidden in the shadows, and when the daughter tries to tell her dad how scary he was, she gets brushed off, grounded, or yelled at, or told not to be a troublemaker.

I agreed to take the guest expert spot because I saw both fathers, the good one and the bad one, and I wanted to somehow speak for both. It is because, I suppose, I always spoke for both in my own father. And because he also, when sober, tried to protect me from the other side of him.

The film clip that went viral was of the drunk dad. It showed David crawling around the floor, slurring his words, trying to eat a hamburger and acting like something that should be put back in its cage. But this view of him was only a part of the picture of fatherhood. There was no footage, for example, of all of the life that went before. There were no clips of the moral, loving dad shown, who would shudder to know what he was doing to his beloved child while drunk, high, and behaving in a way he probably never would when sober.

In a 2007 interview with National Public Radio about his autobiography *Clapton*, famed musician Eric Clapton revealed that at the height of his addiction, he spent about $16,000 on heroin every week. Even when heroin was replaced by alcohol—and frequent cocaine binges— Clapton was unwilling to accept his own addictive tendencies and tried to ignore the problem. At one point, he was so drunk on stage that he performed while lying down because it was the best he could do. During the interview, the now-sober Clapton looked back on this incident saying, "the thing about that kind of addiction that's pretty funny, on reflection, is that I always thought, *I'm handling this. I can handle it. I can stop anytime. I just don't want to stop right now.*"

As children of addicts, we live through these situations of sheer insanity completely sober, with our faculties intact. And we experience the disturbing swings in mood, the bizarre and untethered behavior that accompany addiction, with nothing to numb the pain and terror it engenders. For the addict, there is such a thing as euphoric recall. Not only has the drug altered their memory, it has taken away the horror. But for the child of the addict, there is no such respite. We endure these experiences cold sober. And we are left haunted by memories we tried very, very hard to block. We live with dark shadows floating across our psychic horizon, memories of events and incidents sketched in layers of charcoal, without color or not much, anyway.

We feel embarrassed and ashamed for them and for us. For who knows what? Those feelings "about" them get all mixed up inside of us, and pretty soon we feel those feelings about ourselves. We internalize their shame and wear it as our own, and we shiver every time we get scared, even at a movie.

But then things pop back to a sort of normal, and seem not so bad. We wonder what we were so upset about. Now, all of those feelings we were having have nowhere to go, so we just sit on them or try to forget them. But a part of us knows, and it sits and waits in some corner of our mind for things to get scary again. But then we don't really know we're doing that because—well—we just don't.

This is what the child of an addict experiences. It happens over and over and over again. We are sitting with the parent we know, the dad or mom we have a relationship with, trust, have boundaries with and accept discipline from. And then that parent just sort of goes some-where. Where? No one will really ever know; not even they know, nor will they remember when they sober up. And the person we love becomes creepy, different, and scary. They smell. They talk funny, they move in a weird way, they stumble, they get sloppy, and they make dumb jokes. They come on to our friends. They stop making sense. They alarm and confuse us.

So ACAs see scary things, like people we love transforming into people who freak us out, who terrify us, and who act like they only come alive in the dark—nimble, malevolent, and cold as ice. They are accusing and respect no boundaries. They will say and do anything. They are no longer the people we trust; they have become people who lie and who slip in and out of normal like creatures from a dark beyond.

But they are also our parents, and tomorrow they sober up and have no memory of the labyrinth of blackness that they have dragged us through, and they wonder, "Why does my daughter see me in such a negative way? Why does my son not know that I love him?" And this dark and crazy behavior is absorbed by the family. Eventually the family acts sort of like the drunk person even though they aren't drunk or high. And when they do, *when we do*, we do it with very little awareness of what we are doing or why we are doing it. We have relegated so much that scared us into our unconscious, that when it seeps out, it is still somehow hidden.

But the truth that lives in our body and our unconscious is that *we have a deep and lasting bond with the sober, sane parent, the one we love and feel we know, right alongside our relationship with the creep, the drunk, the narcissist, the liar, and the slob.* And somehow, we figure out, as kids do, how to be with both. *And we model them both,* in fact we often model most astutely the parts of them *that scare us the most.* We model and live out and act out our drunk parent, the one who alarmed us so much that we blocked knowing what we were taking in. Or, the other parent in his or her crazy struggle to keep things going or pretend nothing was happening. And when we live those parts of our parents out, we live them out unconsciously. The very fact that those parts terrified us has rendered them unconscious. Because we were scared, we repressed and split the scary parts of our parents out of our conscious awareness. But they still emerge. They still leak out. We wear them on our faces and in the tone of our voice. We mimic their behavior with an uncanny precision. We march forward into the world, carrying them inside of us.

This is how ACAs pass their unconscious pain along to their children. And when their children try to sort it out, to talk to them about why they got so triggered and acted so weird, the ACAs wonder what they are talking about because we are so out of touch with these pain-filled, rage-filled parts of ourselves. We are unaware that we are unaware, and we can feel very indignant, challenged, and misunderstood if anyone points it out.

Understand that as ACAs, ever the good little, loyal soldiers, we spent our childhoods trying to manage the unmanageable disease of addiction. That means we were trying to manage a drug addict, but they still more or less look like Dad or Mom. So we don't know that this isn't normal; we don't see the illness. Our parent simply keeps acting in strange and frightening or "fun" or smarmy ways. But we keep thinking it's our parent, and our parent keeps using our name and wearing the same clothes and walking through our living room and thus, dragging us into their altered state. We keep trying to relate, to connect, and to find them. Sometimes we get it right, and sometimes we don't, but we keep trying. This becomes a set-up for not knowing what "normal" is, both in a relationship with another person and with our own inner responses. We, too, become out of whack on the inside.

As ACAs, we have been the first responders in a constantly unfolding crisis, always trying to put out fires and manage the chaos and confusion of a family in free fall; picking up dropped balls and making our own school lunches and maybe our kid sisters' and brothers', too. Lying about why our homework isn't done, why our permission slips aren't signed, and why our parent forgot to pick us up or to show up for the class project. Schedules are firm one day and forgotten the next. Missing things becomes routine. Plans fall apart or never happen. And just when we felt we've figured out how to handle the situation, that we had gotten the new family rules of engagement straight, they change all over again, leaving us with a lingering case of emotional vertigo or psychological whiplash.

If we lived with addiction, we lived with dysregulation, with polar-ization—with Dr. Jekyll and Mr. Hyde. The grown-ups in our world were constantly changing before our very eyes. So we may have learned very young not to rely on or trust the people who were supposed to be in charge of us, or maybe worse, to trust them only sometimes (But which times, exactly?). After all, we were little kids making sense of the world with the developmental equipment we had at the time. We loved and needed our parents just to survive. So, because of our proximity and neediness and our deep love and attachment, what went on with our parents went on with us, too. It affected us very deeply. Our parents, simply put, were the most important people in the world to us. They "ran the show"—they *were* the show. So our hearts were constantly being twisted into painful shapes, watching our addicted parent move in and out of reality as we knew it (or thought we knew it) and our other parent trying franticly to keep up appearances, put on a brave face, lie, distort, and deny what is going on right in front of us (or was it?).

Somewhere deep inside, the person who is struggling with a sub-stance use disorder is filled to the brim with shame and self-loathing, even though they would never let themselves *really feel* that. They drink or drug to make the feeling go away. Or they find fault with someone near to them and hold a grudge so long it is impossible to remember what it was about in the first place. They will put someone in the dog-house and deride and devalue them interminably, in an effort to get rid of how bad they feel inside. For a moment, they can smear their shame and self-loathing onto someone else and drag them down to their level, or try to. And we take that in, too. And we act it out. We rage. We blame. We devalue. In an addicted family system, pretty soon everyone starts acting like an addict, even when they are sober. It's dry drunk behavior.

In AA, "dry drunk" is used to describe the behavior of an addict who isn't drinking, who is not using their medication of drugs and alcohol to numb out psychic pain, who is "white knuckling" it. And as ACAs, we model that, too.

ACAs need to bring unconscious material related to the events of their childhood to a conscious level so that it can be processed, understood, and made mature sense of. And this can hurt. It can catapult us back to the most painful parts of our growing up, the parts that we hid from because they hurt too much to feel. They are the parts that we threw out of consciousness because we found them so frightening, and when we re-feel these forgotten emotions, we feel young, vulnerable, and defenseless all over again, just as we did as kids.

And this is why ACAs want to get better in their heads, so we don't have to feel the pain that we carry deep down that we thought we'd left behind. But "out of sight," in this case, is not "out of mind." Our body, our limbic world, carries the fragments of these memories, these shards of our own, personal experience, even if we're unaware of it.

CHAPTER THREE

The Trauma Mind: Not Knowing What Normal Is

It would be impossible to estimate how much time
and energy we invest in trying to fix, change, and deny our
emotions—especially the ones that shake us at our very core,
like hurt, jealousy, loneliness, shame, rage, and grief.

—Debbie Ford

Many of the clients that I treat have never had a problem with substance abuse. But when their, what I like to call, "trauma mind" gets triggered, they still act drunk. Or as we say in the field "dry drunk." Even though there are no alcohol or drugs, they can still think in distorted ways, and their emotional reactions tend to be "black-and-white" alternating between being overly intense or shut down. They have trouble right-sizing their feelings.

Janet Woititz in her seminal book *Adult Children of Alcoholics* was famous for saying, ACAs, "don't know what normal is."

And we don't. *But we don't know that we don't.*

Again and again, I have watched the years and even decades of problems that people make for themselves when they stay unconscious about their childhood pain, simply because they just *don't know what they don't know.* And they don't know *that they don't know.*

ACAs and Intimate Relationships

It's the feelings that *we run from,* that create the most problems for us in our lives and our relationships as adults. It's those emotions that, for whatever reason we want *not to feel,* that we want to deny, minimize, intellectualize, or project, that jam us up on the inside. Because those inner "places and spaces" from the past are always there, vibrating just below the surface of our lives, waiting to be triggered, and with an archer's accuracy, they meet their target, landing straight in the middle of our relationships in the present.

Because the family tried to hide, rewrite, or deny the pain that they were in, it went underground, and that's why for many adult children, it doesn't surface until much later. When we grow up, the very feelings of closeness, dependence, and vulnerability that are a part of any intimate relationship, whether partnering or parenting, trigger old, unresolved, unconscious pain. But the pain that is being triggered was so well defended against in childhood, that we don't know that's what's happening. We think our large, emotional reaction is about who or what triggered it currently, and we aren't able to trace it back to the deeper, younger hurt that is fueling our overreaction.

Because it is relational pain that has remained unprocessed, it is relationships that act as triggers. Relationships become the new target for old pain so that barely conscious pain from the past gets layered onto our present. We stand there six feet tall, using grown up words but operating from a child state. The child inside of us gets warmed up but we don't know that's what's happening. We cannot tolerate what we're feeling, and we cannot understand its origins, so we look for a culprit in real time. We then project our unhealed pain from a time and place in our past, and we make it about our present. But it's at the wrong time and place, with the wrong person, and the wrong names attached to it. In this way, our present becomes hostage to our past.

Needless to say, this complicates relationships. We're shadow-boxing with our past, and we don't even know it. And we don't understand why our reactions are just plain too big—or way too small. Undoing this trauma legacy is the subject of this book.

Remember, ACAs have had an outward person on whom to pin the pathology. Namely the addict. They may have become used to seeing other people as problems and seeing themselves as without issues. This obviously does not help them to get better. In fact, it means that they will likely pass down problematic relational dynamics without awareness simply because they are blind to their own pain. They will not only stay stuck and their early pain will remain unconscious, they will create more relationship issues.

The lifelong complications this creates are not only from the trauma itself, but the way that trauma has taught us to read experience from a fear-based perspective that looks for problems and casts a negative shadow over events. If this trauma is from our childhoods, we have the added problem that our emotional frozenness and fear dates from a time in our lives when we were defenseless and very immature. So, when we get triggered back into this fear and frozenness as an adult, we become immature and overwhelmed in an instant, and we operate from that immature place.

Finding a Path Out

Once I discovered them, just sitting in Al-Anon, ACA, or CODA meetings was deeply transformative for me. Saying what was in my heart and having no one jump up, accuse me of being out of line, slam doors, or rage, changed me in profound ways. No one had ever wanted to hear these things in my family; why should it be any different now? Unconsciously, I expected that as I told my "truth," people might simply gather up their belongings and quietly slip out of the room. I thought that if I shared, the room would just sort of empty out, but it didn't. So this alone was curative for me. It helped me learn to "sit" with my feelings, to feel them without imploding or exploding. I learned to translate those intense feelings into words (create emotional literacy) and share them, which was amazing in and of itself. Then I learned to listen as others shared theirs. As I did this week after week, year after year, my capacity for experiencing intense emotions and thinking about them grew. It was as if my emotional bandwidth got bigger. I had increased capacity because I laid down new neural wiring, though I didn't understand that at the time. And without even knowing it, I embraced recovery—and recovery embraced me.

Over the years, I have had a running conversation with and about ACAs or adult children of relational trauma. These conversations have occurred in my home over a million dinners with friends who "happen to be" ACAs, with a thirty-five-year-long stream of clients, students, and trainees to say nothing of virtually all of my siblings and my siblings-in-law. And of course, my husband. A few themes constantly emerge:

- I feel hypervigilant, I am always waiting for *the other shoe to drop!*
- I get so triggered in my close relationships; I overreact to stuff other people seem to not see as such a big deal.
- Whenever I feel needy, I feel like I am taking up too much space.
- I feel guilty when I say "no" or what I really think or feel.
- I'm not always sure what normal is.
- I can be rigid and controlling sometimes.
- I feel guilty when I take care of myself.
- I am afraid once someone gets to know me, they won't like me.
- I would like to feel angry more, but I feel guilty when I feel angry.
- I self-medicate or I worry that I do.

- I feel like a fake, like an imposter.
- I have a dark side; I ruminate too much on past stuff.
- I felt like our family was different from others.
- I have trouble regulating my emotions.
- I don't trust it when things go too smoothly.

And on the positive side I hear a lot of this:

- I feel deepened by my experiences in life.
- I have a great sense of humor. I love to laugh.
- I am a good manager; somehow, I know what to do in a crisis.
- Because I don't expect everything to be perfect, I can hang and roll with the punches.
- I am independent because I learned not to rely on my parents all the time. I can self-start.
- I can think outside of the box, maybe because I wasn't so sure about "normal" or maybe because I had to from such a young age, before I knew what the box really was.
- I have ingenuity and a creative side.
- I can be very loyal and forgiving.
- I am very intuitive.
- From an early age, I became determined to avoid my parent's pitfalls.
- I just have a sense that my life will work out.
- I love life and get inspired by so many things.
- I know I can manage; I have guts.

It's good to keep in mind that as ACAs, we also gain tremendous strengths and confidence from managing the unmanageable. With the possible exception of Jimmy Carter, all of our past ten presidents have been personally touched by addiction, either being the child or spouse of an alcoholic or having a drinking problem themselves. So being an ACA or a recovering addict certainly doesn't mean we won't be success- ful. In fact it develops unique strengths, ingenuity, doggedness, crea- tivity, and intuition. (Wolin and Wolin)

One of the illuminating discoveries I remember making with my husband was that we each kept a mental "worry list." Each of us upon awakening as teenagers asked ourselves a question that went something like this: "What could go wrong today, or what is already going wrong that I need to be aware of?" This worry list is sort of a sad thing, but it may also have kept us sane, each of us in our own homes. First of all, our awareness that our lives had been turned upside down, meant that they were once more normal. This is lucky; not every ACA has had a period of normalcy. Second, it meant that if we could still identify erratic or dysfunctional behavior; if we could still *see* dysfunction, we had not yet fully adapted to it. Our defensive systems, like denial, repression, intellectualization or rationalization, were not so embedded that we couldn't even see them in operation. Our pain, in other words, wasn't so hidden away under layers of defense that we couldn't feel it. Pain is an indicator that something is wrong, so when we can no longer feel it, we can no longer identify what doesn't feel right. The downside of the worry list however, is that eventually, we need to find a way to let it go. But letting it go can make us feel vulnerable and like we might be blindsided all over again. The worry list was self-protective; it allowed us to anticipate trouble and at least feel a little prepared. But it can become a self-fulfilling prophecy, wherein we actually create problems we're working so hard to avoid.

But the strength that comes out of vulnerability, along with self-knowledge and humility, is awesome. And healing. It opens a path for a different kind of living, both in our intimate relationships and everywhere else in life.

Hope Circuits in the Brain

Martin Seligman and Steven Maier introduced a theory of *learned helplessness* fifty years ago, observing that when animals (and people) encounter situations over which they have no control, they lapse into a state of helplessness. When these situations repeated themselves over time, they developed "learned helplessness," which is a symptom of PTSD. "Today," writes Dwayne Thomas (2017) in "Two New Views of Learned Helplessness":

> Maier and Seligman say that there's more to the story. As their understanding of learned helplessness refined, they found that learned helplessness tended to manifest as one of the following. An inhibited fight flight, in other words feeling trapped and unable to get out of a bad situation. A frozen or thwarted intent towards action, inhibition. Or as exaggerated and overly intense expressions of fear and anxiety. Using this as a starting point, they began to investigate some of the neural circuitry that regulates our fight/flight and fear/anxiety responses. The fear response is activated by a part of the brain connected to both the fight/flight and fear/anxiety circuitry. What they learned essentially was that we have the ability to use our thinking mind, our prefrontal cortex, to inhibit the fear response. And to assess risk and come up with strategies to manage it.

We have choices.

Maier and Seligman named the circuit created between the dorsal raphe nucleus (DRN) and the ventromedial prefrontal cortex (vmPFC) the *hope circuit*, understanding that hope is likely our best defense against helplessness. Hope is defined as the expectation that future bad events will be temporary, local, and controllable. Hope is what the thinking mind can generate when the reptilian or limbic brain/body is calmed down. When we can learn to "sit" with our feelings long enough so that we can begin to think about them. In this simple—but not easy—action we begin to sort out the complexities of our inner world. As feelings rise from their somnolence into the light of consciousness, we can witness them, realizing, *"Oh, that's what was there, and in there all that time. Hmmm.*

Understanding that we have choices, that we have more control over our lives than we think we do, and learning how to strengthen our ability to choose, is core to lasting healing. Positive psychology research makes a compelling observation that most of us will go through painful and challenging circumstances, and most of us will grow from them.

Post-traumatic growth (PTG), a phrase coined by Drs. Richard Tedeschi and Lawrence Calhoun—editors of the *Handbook of Post Traumatic Growth*—names and describes the positive self-transformation that people undergo when they face and deal with the painful or even traumatic experiences in their lives and learn and grow as a result. It refers to a profound, life-altering response to adversity that changes us on the inside as we actively summon the kinds of qualities like fortitude, forgiveness, gratitude, and strength that enable us to not only survive tough circumstances but also thrive. (Dayton, *Neuropsychodrama*)

One of the conundrums of therapy is that it often gives the impression that expressing feelings will automatically lead to their resolution. And when I say that you need to *feel* repressed or dissociated emotions in order to heal them, I realize that I seem to be reinforcing that. But there is a fine line between knowing and expressing them and being stuck in and constantly recycling and relitigating them. The reason we need to feel those emotions that we've blocked out, is so that we can translate them into words and hold them out in the light of our own mind and our relationships so that we can use this beautiful prefrontal cortex, this thinking mind, as the incisive tool that it is—an instrument of logic and understanding. Then we can bring those parts of ourselves that are numb back into a state of sentience and aliveness.

Learned helplessness can morph into a victim mentality, which is not only contagious, it constantly reproduces itself. It stops growth in its tracks. When we get stuck in helplessness and hopelessness, we lose our ability to perceive choices. There is nothing wrong with coming to terms with having been victimized; it's a part of the healing process, however we just don't want helplessness and victimhood to settle in as an identity. So if you are asking the question "Why me?" just remember to ask, "Why not me?" People go through wars, despots, camps, torture, and a myriad of other terrifying things. You can go through relational trauma *and recovery*.

So What Blocks Recovery?

As a clinician, I worry much less about the ACA who comes into treatment emotionally bleeding or really feeling their painful emotions once they become aware of them, than the one who comes in thinking they are fine but has complaints about their spouse or their children. When they come in "on their knees," as we say in twelve-step programs, they come in humble and ready to change and grow. When they come in for "someone else," they may be coming in deeply defended and having located their unresolved pain not within themselves but within another family member who they have labeled "the problem."

As we said earlier, as ACAs we can be unaware of the pain we carry around. Our own overreactions and problems with self-regulation may catch us off guard. We ACAs are often smart, resourceful, and competent, and we can't see why this recovery thing should be so complex and take so long. And we have a lifelong habit of avoiding pain, pushing it down and explaining it away. We often want to think ourselves better, to get better in our heads, bypassing years and years of the cumulative effects of relational trauma. We feel that if we *understand* what happened, we should be over it.

So ACAs and adult children sometimes:

Don't Want to Feel Vulnerable. Because of the deep defenses that ACAs have developed to keep their own internal pain and hurt from being known to them, to keep it out of consciousness, recovery can feel just too painful. And pointless. We feel at risk, as if the therapist is digging around where they don't belong or asking us to feel things that are better off remaining in the past. Pain was split off so consistently that *going there* is just too scary. We worry that there will be no bottom, that we'll go there and never find our way back out again. We feel like we've been victimized twice, one as a defenseless child who got hurt and now as an adult who's stuck dealing with it.

Have a Desire for a Quick Fix. ACAs can feel resentful about the time and money they realize they need in order to recover. We resent that years and years of pain can't be healed in a week, or a year. We think, "If they were the addict, why am I stuck with the damage, and why am I the one who needs to recover? Not fair! I am not going to! This may be a part of why ACAs want a quick fix: "I'm good enough, I'm not in crisis, I just need to understand a few things then I'll be all better." While resentment is a perfectly normal feeling, we need to get past it and see doing the work of recovery as a caring and self-affirming act. We need to do it because we value our happiness more than our resentment. And we need to develop an in-depth understanding of how trauma affects the mind/body so that we can be patient with ourselves.

Have Difficulty Asking for Help. ACAs have learned that asking for help can be a bad idea. For one thing, we may have gotten vastly different answers depending on the day or moment we asked. We may have been ridiculed or told we were being "dramatic." Or, we were made to feel like we were a real mess. Maybe there was no one "there" to even notice that we were asking. Because of this, we may, over time, lose the ability to feel our own neediness. It got us nowhere if not into trouble to feel it as kids, so we learned to shut that part of us down. This can mean that we don't know when or even that we need help, and we may see ourselves as weak or even stupid for needing it. We may feel we're taking up a lot of space in asking for help or that we'll open up, only to be told we're too much. We fear that if we let ourselves need it, it will only lead to more disappointment when it disappears again, because at some level, that is what we expect.

Have Trouble Accepting Support. ACAs can have trouble taking in caring and support from others. (van der Kolk 2005) We may fear that if we let support in, we'll owe something to anyone who is being nice to us or that if we let support feel good, it will only be taken away eventually, and we'll hurt all the more, having opened up. Remember as ACAs, we learn to figure things out on our own—to not lean, need, or expect, or we learn to get our needs met surreptitiously. So the whole "getting our needs met" thing can be very confusing, as we've learned to shut them down or to meet them in less than functional ways.

Have Trouble Processing New Information. ACAs can also have a hard time taking in new information, especially when we're stuck in what I call our "trauma minds." When we're in our "trauma mind," we're locked into a defensive position, a position originally developed to ward off deep feelings of vulnerability and fear. Our thinking mind is shutting down, so taking in new information becomes very difficult; we don't necessarily hear and process it. Or, we're triggered and in that state of reliving our trauma, we're deeply preoccupied and unavailable to take in new information. This is where twelve-step programs can be a real godsend. Just sitting and listening to others share can bring up a lot of vulnerability but it does so gradually, and in a good and healthy meeting, there should be no pressure to share and no cross talk. This gives those with PTSD time; *time* to learn to tolerate intense emotions without imploding or exploding; *time* to get used to feeling again, rather than being numb, shut down, or dissociated; and *time* to learn just to sit with feelings and witness them as they roll around inside of us.

Don't Know What Normal Is. ACAs don't know what normal is; we have, in fact, often normalized chaos and abuse. We may honestly have a hard time conceptualizing "normal," or we may think that normal is boring, prosaic, or lacks imagination. We may even have idealized our version of "not normal," seeing it as creative, out of the box, or superior to the majority of people who are living dull and lackluster lives. However, kids *need* normal, they need dependability and predictability in order to organize their lives and their minds, and manage their moods and their expectations. And if ACAs find living within a more normal range somehow threatening to their sense of themselves, that in and of itself needs to be looked at.

Are in Denial. While I always encourage looking on the bright side and reframing situations to see them in their best possible light, we need to be aware of our own tendency to deny or rewrite reality to make it more palatable.

Denial is a refusal to accept a situation that is causing pain and chaos for what it is. It is a rewriting of reality to make it less painful. It is considered one of the most primitive of the defense mechanisms, and it can be very difficult to penetrate because it is stubborn and immature. An alcoholic may deny that they have a drinking problem and point out that they function well at work and, that they only drink at certain times of the day. Their spouse may join in their denial by stretching out the cocktail hour and dinner so that they have plenty of time to drink, making excuses for them, or pretending to themselves that this is somehow normal—and that "everyone does it." Whatever form denial takes, it can keep us from seeing what is going on around us and "protect" us both from the pain of it and the feeling that we should do something about it. Denial can also keep us from making contact with our inner world.

Are Stuck in Our Reptilian Brain. Our primitive brain is wired to scan for danger. This is at the base of what psychologists refer as a *negativity bias.* If humans, animals, and reptiles weren't programmed to notice and read danger, we wouldn't still be here. It's natural to want to self-protect. This part of us can, however, get in the way of taking risks and trying new things. And recovery does feel like a risk. It asks us to go to places within ourselves that feel dangerous, painful, and scary. This negativity bias can just pour out excuse after excuse as to why we shouldn't take a deeper look into ourselves.

Esther Perel, author of *Mating in Captivity,* talks about the community of first-generation Holocaust survivors that she grew up with in Belgium. She says that those who survived the camps fell into two broad groups: (1) the group that went on living; and (2) the group that came back to life.

Our minds are meaning-makers. We all need to make sense out of our own experience: this is a function of the thinking mind. We are the interpreters of the circumstances of our lives because we are the ones living inside our own heads. We can choose to see the events and circumstances of our lives as dark and senseless or as stepping stones on a path toward enlightenment. Seeing recovery as a path or a foundation through which we can learn to build a better, freer, and more purposeful life can be part of how we author our own story. We write as we go, so write a good story, because it's yours to write.

Working with Emotions: Processing My Feelings

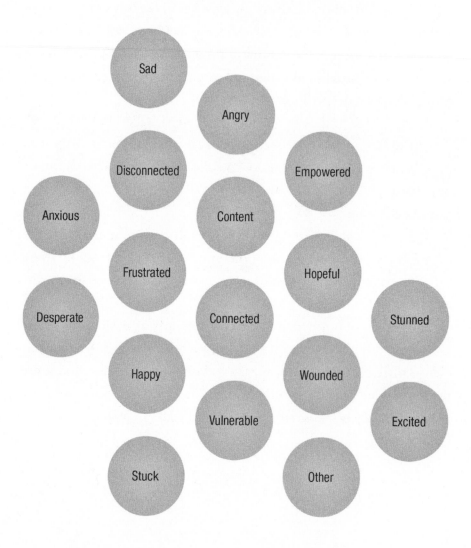

Think of situations that trigger you. Glance over the circles and see what word or words draw you in. Share about why you think they popped out at you.

_____

_____

_____

_____

In what part of your body do you feel this feeling? Describe the physical sensations, if any, that accompany the feeling.

_____

_____

_____

_____

How do you breathe at moments when you are feeling like this? And how do you imagine breathing like this affects the way that you think and act?

_____

_____

_____

_____

What are your associations with this feeling, i.e. people, places, and things? Describe them briefly.

_____

_____

_____

_____

What situations trigger this feeling in you? And once the feeling is triggered, how do you handle the situation?

_____

_____

Do you have images in your mind of how others see you at these moments? If so, what do you imagine others might be thinking?

Can you trace this feeling to early in your life? If so, describe where you think this feeling may have set in.

If this feeling had a color, what would it be? If this feeling had a smell, what would it be? If this feeling had a shape, what would it be? If this feeling had a sound, what would it be? If this feeling had a texture, what would it be? If this feeling had a taste, what would it be?

How do you feel when you encounter this feeling in others?

When you experience anxiety or fear, what tools, if any, do you draw on to manage it?

_____

_____

_____

_____

Name a situation in which you felt you had managed this set of feelings well.

_____

_____

_____

_____

How did you feel, think, and act when you felt you'd managed well?

_____

_____

_____

_____

Is there any advice you might give to another person who struggles with this?

_____

_____

_____

_____

Is there any advice you'd give to yourself next time you encounter this feeling?

_____

_____

_____

_____

CHAPTER FOUR

Adverse Childhood Experiences: Can Childhood Trauma Make Us Sick?

"This [ACE's] story is game-changing, the most important
public health study you've never heard of."

—Oprah Winfrey

"In the mid-nineties the Center for Disease Control (CDC) discovered an exposure that dramatically increases the risk for seven out of ten, of the leading causes of death, in the United States. In high doses, it affects brain development, the immune system, the hormonal system and even the way our DNA is read and transcribed. Folks who are exposed in very high doses have triple the lifetime risk of heart disease and lung cancer and a twenty-year difference in life expectancy. And yet doctors today are not trained in routine screening or treatment," says Dr. Nadine Burke Harris author of *The Deepest Well: Healing the Long-Term Effects of Childhood Adversity* and current California Surgeon General in her TED Talk, "Now the exposure I'm talking about is not a pesticide or a packaging chemical. It's childhood trauma. I'm

41

not talking about failing a test or losing a basketball game. I am talking about threats that are so severe or pervasive that they literally get under our skin and change our physiology, things like abuse or neglect or growing up with a parent who struggles with mental illness or substance dependence, *adverse childhood experiences*."

The Adverse Childhood Experiences (ACE) study, led by Robert F. Anda, MD, MS of the CDC; Vincent Feletti, MD; and David W. Brown, DSc, MScPH, MSc, in 2006 is one of the largest studies ever conducted on the relationship between trauma in childhood and long-term effects on health and well-being. It draws an irrefutable connection between childhood trauma and health problems, both physical and mental, later in life.

The study included more than 17,000 health maintenance organization (HMO) members who underwent a comprehensive physical examination that provided detailed information about their childhood experiences of abuse, neglect, and family dysfunction. The researchers were not looking toward family addiction as a unique risk factor in their study design. But as they gathered data, parental addiction and the dysfunctional behaviors that clustered around it kept emerging *as one of the statistically most significant causes of mental, emotional, and physical health problems in adulthood.* ACAs, in other words, continue to experience the effects of growing up with addiction throughout their lives.

Dr. Harris has also made a connection between adverse childhood experiences and Attention Deficit Hyperactivity Disorder (ADHD).

> While the most common diagnosis for kids with attention and behavior issues is Attention Deficit Hyperactivity Disorder, or ADHD, Burke Harris found that many of the kids who might normally receive this label had experienced high levels of adverse childhood experiences, or ACEs, from extreme poverty and exposure to violence, to neglect or living with a parent who suffered from addiction to drugs or alcohol. (Brie Zeltner *The Plain Dealer*)

Harris chose to work in a low-income, primarily minority community. Even with children who grew up in a situation that might be seen as disadvantaged, Burke found that only 3 percent of the children in her practice experienced behavior and learning problems when they had no exposure to trauma. "Our children are not broken.... these kids' behavior was a direct result of toxic doses of the adversity they were experiencing." Without an exposure to ACE's, her kids learned well.

Learning requires that we *attend* to what's going on in the moment so that we're calm and present enough to listen and learn. It also requires that the thinking part of our mind is awake and aware; we need to be able to think and attend in order to learn. Trauma can shut down our prefrontal cortex; in times of terror or stress, the thinking mind goes offline. This shutting down of the thinking mind naturally affects a child's ability to take in and understand new information, to learn. Relational trauma can also teach kids not to trust. Learning requires that we connect to another person. If kids learn that connection is anxiety provoking and if they fear criticism or even brace for pain, it may affect their ability to be comfortable and teachable. And it may make them suspicious of those who want to help them.

One of the beginnings of the ACE Study dates from Vincent Felitti's weight-loss program at Kaiser Permanente. (1985) Frustrated and puzzled by the number of the people in his program, who dropped out even though they were losing weight successfully, he began to look more deeply into their personal histories. Upon investigation, Felitti discovered that many people in his clinic had experienced physical and sexual abuse growing up. When he questioned them further, his participants talked about how their feelings of anxiety that emerged after significant weight loss, were driving them to drop out of the program and regain the weight. People in the study reported that their weight felt like "protection." Once they lost weight, they felt vulnerable and exposed; it created new fear that they'd be attractive and that felt somehow "dangerous." Through the lens of addiction, we see that when their "medicator," namely food, was removed, the fears that they were medicating felt all the more intense. Without help in processing those feelings so that they could be understood and moved through and, so that they could develop their own skills of mood management and self-regulation rather than use food to do that for them, they relapsed.

A similar phenomenon can be seen in drug and alcohol treatment. Years ago, we felt that it was too risky for addicts, who were getting sober from drugs and alcohol, to work with their childhood trauma while in treatment. But over time, it became evident that not working with it was also risky because unresolved trauma could become the pain pump that fueled relapse. The emotional and psychological pain that may have led someone to self-medicate in the first place, in other words, was not only still there when they got sober, it hurt all the more because they were no longer using drugs and alcohol to numb it out. So addicts are oftentimes using drugs and alcohol to obliterate the pain of growing up with childhood trauma or ACEs. This is the connection between trauma and addiction.

ACEs Cluster

Early on, Anda and Feletti were simply looking at what factors drove up health care costs. What made people go to the doctor more often and make claims on their insurance? Through collating reams of data, it emerged that growing up with emotionally and psychologically painful or traumatizing experiences, was one of the strongest predictors of health problems later in life. Hence, the coining of the term *adverse childhood experiences* or ACE factors.

It also became evident that parental addiction is a gateway for many forms of toxic stress. If a child grows up with addiction, that is probably not the only risk factor in the home because *ACEs tend to cluster.* "Once a home environment is disordered, the risk of witnessing or experiencing emotional, physical, or sexual abuse actually rises dramatically," says Anda. Addiction, not surprisingly, is statistically correlated with neglect, verbal, emotional, physical, or sexual abuse. Alcohol and drugs reduce inhibitions and impair judgement in the user, making it more likely that their inhibitions against certain behaviors are diminished. A father who would condemn sexual abuse while sober, for instance, may abuse his children when drunk. Rage in the home is more likely as family members are filled with humiliation and hurt and feel helpless to improve the situation. Emotional neglect is virtually baked into the family system.

The intense moodiness that accompanies addiction, whether effusive or abusive, creates the kind of chaos in the family that impacts everyone. And the sober parent, if there is one, is often too overwhelmed to pick up the slack, or remain on the job in the way they might have, were both parents functioning normally. Normalcy, in fact, goes out the window. The parents are no longer team players because one member of the team checks out and acts out, and the other family members are left to fill in, as best they can. But they themselves are oftentimes hurt and resentful, are not talking about what is going on, and basically, they are running on empty. And they may have their own psychological issues. Because of the slow degradation that surrounds addiction, family members become increasingly traumatized. It takes increasingly less to trigger them into an overreaction. And these are, generally speaking, not families who talk about their experiences and find relief. Consequently, stress goes underground, and emotions get repressed. According to Gabor Maté, MD, in *When the Body Says No*:

> When emotions are repressed…this inhibition disarms the body's defenses against illness. Repression-dissociating emotions from conscious awareness and relegating them to the unconscious realm, disorganizes

and confuses our physiological defenses so that in some people, these defenses go awry, becoming the destroyers of health, rather than its protectors." (Maté p. 7)

Painful childhood experiences that don't get handled at the time or near the time they occur can morph into what Harvard researchers call *toxic stress* and can impact all health issues across the board, physical and mental, and they dramatically increase the number of visits to the doctor. Health care costs skyrocket, which was the impetus for this study in the first place. Although people are going to the doctor for physical ailments, anything from chronic back problems, gastrointestinal issues, heart problems, and so forth, the ACE study made clear that there is a significant connection between childhood pain and health problems later in life. So, if we want our health care costs to go down, we need to begin in childhood. According to the Center on the Developing Child at Harvard University (2015):

> The toxic stress response can occur when a child experiences strong, frequent, and/or prolonged adversity—such as physical or emotional abuse, chronic neglect, caregiver substance abuse or mental illness, exposure to violence, and/or the accumulated burdens of family economic hardship—without adequate adult support. This kind of prolonged activation of the stress response systems can disrupt the development of brain architecture and other organ systems, and increase the risk for stress-related disease and cognitive impairment, well into the adult years.

When Our Inner World Shuts Down

The nature of psychic trauma is that we do not feel it when it is happening. We block shocking pain, terrifying moments, or what hurts too much. It's self-protective. If, soon after a painful moment happens, we can come back around and feel those feelings that we shut down, we'll process those we put on hold, take in comfort and caring from someone, and we'll move along. But if those feelings never get felt or seen or understood or cared about, they will live in hiding inside of us. Unresolved trauma is like yeast in the mind, it grows, and it develops a half-life. Then rather than minimize a difficulty, the trauma mind maximizes it, loads it up with all sorts of fear and blame and shame-based emotion that makes it get larger.

Here's What Happens…

When we're terrified, our thinking mind shuts down so that our fight-or-flight system can work unencumbered. Nature doesn't want us thinking about whether or not to get out of harm's way; it just wants us to react fast. Those split seconds can mean the critical difference between life or death. But our limbic brain/body (read: fight/flight/freeze) that is responsible for processing our emotions and sense impressions continues to gather data like sights, sounds, smells. However, there are huge gaps in our recollection of events because the part of our brain that would have made sense of the situation, namely the prefrontal cortex—the part of us that thinks and reasons and creates meaning—was shut down. Offline. Our thinking is suspended but our limbic world is highly activated, we're busily scanning for danger and recording the sights, sounds, sensations and so forth of the experience but we're not thinking about what is going on, that part of us is temporarily not functioning.

Body Memories

But the body remembers, it holds onto bits and pieces of the memories even though the mind "forgets," that's what body memories are all about. So we're left with fragments of experiences, bits and pieces of the story, and flashes of feelings that we can't quite attach to anything specific; we have no storyline that pulls together these disparate pieces and makes relevant sense and meaning of them and puts them into a context in our lives. This results later in our inability to attach the right word to what we're feeling.

We need to feel our feelings and elevate them to a conscious level through words and thought so our bodies don't have to hold them for us. Emotional trauma can manifest in our bodies as headaches, back aches, muscle tightness, soreness and weariness. It can also become the kind of toxic stress that develops into illness. Our body in these cases is trying to tell us something that we need to listen to.

If the relational trauma that is at the root of this dysregulation is attachment related, that is, if we grow up with abuse and/or neglect and this happens month after month and occurs at the hands of those we love and depend upon, those with whom we have formed our most primary and primitive attachments, then our stress and dysregulation may become chronic and toxic.

Dr. Anda describes why ongoing, traumatic experiences can have such tenacious effects:

> For an epidemic of influenza, a hurricane, earthquake, or tornado, the worst is quickly over; treatment and recovery efforts can begin. In contrast, the chronic disaster that results from ACEs is insidious and constantly rolling out from generation to generation. If the effects of toxic stress are not understood, so that children can receive some sort of understanding and support from home, school and community, these children simply vanish from view...and randomly reappear—as if they are new entities—in all of your service systems later in childhood, adolescence and adulthood as clients with behavioral, learning, social, criminal, and chronic health problems. (Anda, Felitti, et al., 2006)

People with high ACE scores, who experienced the cumulative effect of growing up with a cluster of adverse childhood experiences, tended to be those who fell into the healthcare and penal systems in adulthood. The study suggests their childhood stress was more than their brain/body could process (Anda, Felitti, et al., 2006). According to Dr. Anda, growing up with ACEs causes pain and also carries a higher risk for other issues, including having risky sexual behavior; STDs; contracting HIV from injected drug use; suffering from pulmonary disease; smoking-related lung disease; autoimmune disease; poor adolescent health; teen pregnancy; and mental health issues. Or, on the relationship front, ACEs can lead to revictimization, instability of relationships, and possibly poor performance in school or in the workforce. These are the kids that get sick more often, who get into trouble, and who are "at risk."

Dr. Bessel van der Kolk, who was on the initial task force to create a diagnosis for PTSD to put into the *Diagnostic and Statistical Manual of Mental Disorders, Fourth Edition* (DSM-IV), refers to how the politics of establishing the diagnosis took attention off of some of the most basic manifestations of PTSD. "The impact of pervasive trauma in our society continues to be largely ignored. We know today that one out of eight kids in the U.S. has been a victim of maltreatment, and that half of all kids in the world are exposed to extreme violence. The Adverse Childhood Experiences studies have demonstrated that early exposure to family violence and emotional abuse is the largest and costliest public health issue in America. As a society, we mobilize against threats like ISIS, but most American kids are not the victims of foreign terrorists; they're the victims of the social conditions in which they mature."

When we say "social conditions," we are referring to the family and the community that a child matures in. What kind of parenting did they receive? How solid was their family structure? Did they have extended family, a safe neighborhood, and decent schools? What was the atmosphere around their dinner table; was it stable, with parents who tuned into them, took care of them, and were concerned about their day?

How were they raised in the early years? And on the more subtle end of this, did their parents help them to love themselves or was there a subtle tyranny or temper, criticism, and emotional abuse? We focus on physical and sexual abuse as the types that devastate us. But I have found that treating adult children who have been criticized, neglected, or manipulated for someone else's purposes can be difficult to get to and change. The drip, drip, drip of emotional abuse has wrapped itself so thoroughly around their identity that it is hard to understand and clearly see.

When childhood needs are not well met, it becomes not only expensive but incredibly difficult for public health institutions to intervene and fix the problem. How children were raised creates the foundation for who they will become.

Van der Kolk continues to explain the confusion around how we see PTSD, "through a hard-fought political process, involving veterans organizations and mental health professionals, the diagnosis of PTSD eventually was created in 1980. Part of the politics of the process was that we had to make that direct link between vets' struggles and their combat experiences. Hence, we focused on nightmares and flashbacks—intrusive memories of traumatic combat experiences— while downplaying problems with emotional engagement and emotion regulation, issues that we gradually came to understand as being the result of trauma changing fundamental brain processes. To this day, the PTSD diagnosis focuses on having unpleasant memories of the past, rather than on emotion regulation and having problems fully engaging in the present."

Anda feels that society has bought into some myths concerning adverse childhood experiences, such as, "ACEs are rare, that they happen somewhere else, that they are perpetrated by monsters, that some, or maybe most, children can escape unscathed, or if not that they can be rescued and healed by emergency response systems." If we leave it up to our public health systems to treat kids or adults who are already in trouble, we will make the job infinitely more difficult. We need to look at parenting styles, family composition, educational systems, and the environment at home and in the neighborhood.

A Trauma-Inducing Environment

In his book *In an Unspoken Voice,* Dr. Peter Levine refers to a study done in Israel by Dr. Riehshaleev. The study was conducted in an emergency room where heartbeats are routinely taken upon entry. In Israel, they are characteristically high, which may not be surprising given the environmental emergency-type stresses that may have led to patients being hospitalized.

The doctors found that if the patient's heartbeat was lower at the time of dismissal, the chances of that person developing PTSD were less high. Dr. Levine goes on to explain that when we are terrified, the body goes into fight/flight mode; we are flooded with stress-related chemicals that will allow us to flee for safety or stand and fight. If these chemicals aren't used up, the heart rate remains high, and the body doesn't restore its homeostasis. Heart rate is a direct window into the autonomic nervous system. A racing heart is part of the body and mind, readying for the survival action of fight or flight and mediated by the sympathetic adrenal nervous system. "When we perceive threat our nervous system and body prepare to kill or to take evasive countermeasures to escape usually by running away. This preparation for action was absolutely essential on the ancient savannas and it was discharged or used up by all our meaningful action," says Dr. Levine. "If rather than feeling and fulfilling these motoric actions and discharging them, this preparation for action gets interfered with, say by your head lying dormant, [or being strapped down] it would pose a great potential to trigger a later expression of the debilitating symptoms of a post-traumatic stress disorder."

Dr. Levine goes on to describe the body's need to "shake, rattle and roll, to shiver and quiver" as a means of its self-regulating and returning back to normal. This is what animals in the wild do if and when they have been locked into a helpless state say by being tranquilized, caged, or tied if they have been confined. Levine cites a rather astonishing example given by an African wildlife zookeeper. The zookeeper described that if the animals they released back into the wild do not go through this shivering and shaking process, they will generally not survive. It will have interfered with their resilience, their natural path back into a self-regulated state or their ability to be frightened and to move through a process of releasing the fight/flight chemicals in their body. Without their regulation restored, their ability to spontaneously react to danger, to defend themselves, or to release the energy and eventually return to a normal or self-regulated state will be so impaired that they cannot survive. So shaking is the body's way of restoring itself and returning to normal. It is the body's way of remaining resilient in the face of the inevitable and continued threat that is part of life. But all too often, we see this shivering and shaking as pathological, and we try to stop it either by medicating someone, by giving them shots to quiet down, or by telling them to relax and calm down. However, *it is this natural process that allows the body to restore itself; to return to a state of equilibrium and resilience.*

How We Lose Our Ability
to Calm Down and Self-Soothe

Children who are being abused are deprived of their fight/flight are trapped in the moment, and if they try to defend themselves, they are generally abused even more, so they are not able to either burn off their fight/flight chemicals or to "shiver and quiver" to release them. Over time, this can interfere with their finding their way back to "normal," to emotional regulation, and to homeostasis, all of which can interfere with what would otherwise be their natural resilience.

The limbic system governs such fundamental aspects of self as mood, appetite, and sleep cycles. Dysregulation in the limbic system can manifest as difficulty in regulating eating, sleep, mood, depression, or anxiety. It can lead to a desire to self-medicate, to use something outside of ourselves as a source of mood regulation because we can't regulate on our own, which we'll go into further in our chapter on process addictions.

The more we self-medicate to manage our emotional dysregulation, the more we become dependent on these kinds of solutions to calm down. And the weaker our ability to calm ourselves down, to self-soothe, to just be becomes. Then the more we use and abuse.

NOTE: On the next page you will find the Relational Trauma Symptom List that I have developed over the years. I would also like to direct you to *tiandayton.com/soulfuljourney* so that you can take The Adverse Childhood Experiences Inventory along with the Resilience Inventory. You may find that even though you may have a high ACE Score, you may also have a high Resilience Score that has helped you to cope successfully!

The Relational Trauma Symptom List

Anxiety/Hypervigilance (van der Kolk):	Hypervigilance has to do with being overly sensitized to stress, it can include an exaggerated startle response or a "hair trigger". We may scan our environment and relationships for signs of perceived relationship insults and ruptures. We may over read signs from others, Members of addicted, abusive or neglectful families may "wait for the other shoe to drop", or "walk on eggs shells," feeling that danger is around the corner.
Tendency to Isolate/ Withdraw/Avoid:	People who have experienced relational trauma may see avoiding certain subjects or deep connection with others as a way of saving themselves from further pain, they isolate and withdraw.
Unresolved Grief:	It is difficult to feel and heal what we are afraid to bring to a conscious level. As a result, the relational dynamics that hurt us most tend to be those that we repress and deny, consequently we don't heal that old pain, it remains hidden inside of us.
Loss of Trust and Faith (van der Kolk):	When our personal world and the relationships within it become too unpredictable and unreliable, we may experience a loss of trust and faith in relationships, an orderly and predictable world, as well as in life's ability to repair and renew itself.
Easily Triggered/Intense Emotional Reactions:	We over respond to relational stress, blowing conflicts that could be managed, out of proportion into unmanageability, particularly if we are feeling vulnerable. We become over sensitized to stress, we over react to it. intimidate others, or shut down and freeze. (van der Kolk, van der Hart, Burbridge)
Numbing of responsiveness/ Emotional Constriction:	Numbness and shutdown as a defense against overwhelming pain. Restricted range of affect or lack of authentic expression of emotion. "Aware of their difficulties in controlling their emotions, traumatized people seem to spend their energies on the avoiding of distressing internal sensations, instead of attending to the demands of the environment. In addition, they loose satisfaction in matters that previously gave them a sense of satisfaction and may feel "dead to the world". This emotional numbing may be expressed as depression, as anhedonia and lack of motivation, as psychosomatic reactions, or as dissociative states." (van der Kolk, van der Hart, Burbridge)

© *Tian Dayton, PhD, TEP. Permission to reprint granted with the following attribution: Published in* The Soulful Journey of Recovery, *Health Communications, Inc., 2019.*

Problems with Self-Regulation:	We go from 0–10 and 10–0 without intermediate stages, no shades of gray, we cycle back and forth between extreme ranges of functioning and intense emotional reactions. The loss of neuromodulation or the ability to self regulate, that is at the core of PTSD leads to loss of affect regulation. "Traumatized people go immediately from stimulus to response without being able to first figure out what makes them so upset. They tend to experience intense fear, anxiety, anger and panic in response to even minor stimuli. This makes them either overreact or withdraw".
Shame:	Living with trauma and/or addiction can engender bad feelings about ourselves. Especially when the trauma in the home is a part of a child's young and naturally egocentric years. Young children tend to make everything about themselves, including their parent's pain, they can internalize a sense of being at fault and this can engender shame.
Development of Rigid Psychological Defenses:	People who are being wounded emotionally and are not able to address it openly and honestly may develop rigid psychological defenses to manage their fear and pain. Dissociation, denial, splitting, repression, minimization, intellectualization, projection are some examples.
Distorted Reasoning:	When our family unit is spinning out of control, we will tell ourselves whatever is necessary to allow ourselves to stay connected. This kind of reasoning can be immature and distorted. It can also produce core beliefs about life and relationships upon which we build more distorted reasoning and that we live out throughout our lives. Additionally small children create meaning with the developmental equipment available to them at any given age. Their meaning may be, for this reason, immature, distorted or may include "magical" interpretations of life events.
Depression:	The limbic system regulates mood. When we are disregulated in our limbic world we may have trouble regulating feelings such as anger, sadness and fear, all of which may contribute to depression. *And high levels of coritosol which are associated with the fight/flight response (which is associated with trauma) are also found in high amounts in people who report feeling depressed.*

© Tian Dayton, PhD, TEP. Permission to reprint granted with the following attribution: Published in The Soulful Journey of Recovery, Health Communications, Inc., 2019.

Relationship Issues:	Relationship trauma occurs in relationships as the name implies. Relationships tend also to be where the effects of relationship trauma reemerge. Some of the ways in which trauma related issues reemerge are being easily triggered, bringing old patterns into new relationships (reenactment patterns), transferencing old pain onto partners, children, friends or authority figures, being hyper vigilant hence creating an emotional atmosphere of anxiety and suspicion or being easily triggered hence creating instability within the relationship and unnecessary pain.
Desire to Self Medicate:	A loss of ability to regulate moods naturally applies to substances and behaviors as well. These are misguided attempts to quiet and control a turbulent, troubled inner world through the use of drugs and alcohol or behavioral addictions.
Body/Somatic Disturbances/Sleep Problems:	Our body sometimes does our feeling for us if we can't feel and heal it consciously Emotion gets stored in a sensitive body part, we get tight muscles, back problems, queasiness, chronic headaches and so on. Or we may experience sleep problems, flashbacks that intrude on our relaxation or nightmares.
Learned Helplessness:	When we feel we can do nothing to affect or change the situation we're in, we may develop what's called, learned helplessness, we may have trouble moving out of the collapse that can be part of the natural trauma response.
Learning difficulties:	The ability to attend in the present can be negatively impacted by trauma. Physiological hyperarousal interferes with the capacity to concentrate and to attend in the present and to make sense of, draw meaning from and learn from experience or teaching. (van der Kolk, van der Hart, Burbridge)
Cycles of Reenactment:	The reenactment dynamic is one of the core features of how trauma from one generation gets passed down through subsequent generations. We tend to recreate those circumstances in our lives that feel unresolved or unconscious.
Loss of Ability to Take in caring and support from others (van der Kolk):	The numbing response, along with the emotional constriction that are part of the trauma response, may lead to a loss of ability to take in caring and support from others. Additionally, as mistrust grows, so does our willingness to accept love and support.

© Tian Dayton, PhD, TEP. Permission to reprint granted with the following attribution: Published in The Soulful Journey of Recovery, Health Communications, Inc., 2019.

High Risk Behaviors (van der Kolk)**:**	The clients that I see who are engaged in chronic high risk behaviors seem to be trying to do a couple of things. One, they seem to be trying to jump start a numbed out inner world, to feel *something*. Or they appear to be acting out intense emotional and psychological pain. Another dynamic that appears to be operating, is that they are trying to alter their mood, that the hi risk behavior serves to get them into an altered state through a rush of adrenaline which is as addictive to the brain as heroin. Speeding, sexual acting out, spending, fighting, drugging or other behaviors done in a way that puts one at risk are some examples of high risk behaviors.
Aggression against self and others:	"Being abused as a child sharply increases the risk for later delinquency and violent criminal behavior. In one study of 87 psychiatric outpatients (van der Kolk et al.,1991) we found that self-mutilators invariably had severe childhood histories of abuse and/or neglect. There is good evidence that selfmutilative behavior is related to endogenous opioid changes in the CNS secondary to early traumatization." (van der Kolk, van der Hart, Burbridge)
Survival Guilt:	The person who "gets out" of an unhealthy family system while others remain mired within it may experience what is referred to as 'survivor's guilt."
Traumatic Bonding:	Traumatic bonds, may develop between parent and child or among siblings. Siblings in alcoholic homes may be left to care for each other, older siblings may have power over their younger siblings and be immature care takers or one parent may co-opt a particular child to meet their unmet needs for intimacy and support.
False Self Functioning:	Creating a "false self" that is more acceptable to others rather than being your authentic self. A presentation that you imagine will work better in your family system but does not allow you to be your authentic self. The concept of false self came from D. W. Winnecott who used the term "true or real self to describe a sense of self based on spontaneous authentic experience, and a feeling of being alive". He saw the false self as a "defensive façade, lacking spontaneity and feeling dead and empty, behind a mere appearance of being real."

© Tian Dayton, PhD, TEP. Permission to reprint granted with the following attribution: Published in The Soulful Journey of Recovery, *Health Communications, Inc., 2019.*

Relational Trauma
Symptom List Reflections

Look over this symptom list and answer the following questions:

1. Which characteristics pop out at you as those you identify with? Put them in order here:

_____

_____

_____

_____

_____

2. Which of these characteristics do you feel you struggle with the most? Choose two or three and write a little about that.

_____

_____

_____

_____

_____

_____

3. Which of these characteristics do you see other family members that you grew up with struggle with? Name the person and the symptom and say a little bit about that.

_____

_____

_____

_____

_____

4. Which of these symptoms are in your way when it comes to recovery? Name them and describe why.

_____

_____

_____

_____

_____

5. Which of these symptoms did you used to deal with but you have come a long way in getting through it/them? What are they and describe how you learned to master it.

_____

_____

_____

_____

_____

_____

_____

_____

CHAPTER FIVE

In the Arms of Those Who Raise Us: Trauma, Love, and Attachment

A deep sense of love and belonging is an irreducible
need of all people. We are biologically, cognitively, physically,
and spiritually wired to love, to be loved, and to belong.
When those needs are not met, we don't function as we were
meant to. We break. We fall apart. We numb.
We ache. We hurt others. We get sick.

—Brené Brown

A particular challenge for ACAs and children of adverse childhood experiences is that the trauma they experience is often caused by their caregivers, who are the very people they'd normally turn to for comfort and protection.

Our nervous systems are built to attune and resonate with the nervous systems of others so that we can achieve a sense of balance and regulation within the context of a relationship connection (Schore, 1999). Our neurological wiring is not completely formed at birth. Each tiny interaction between parent and child continues to lay down and strengthen our neural wiring, which helps us to "hold" emotion and sensation and regulate it. *If we fail to find a sense of resonance and safety in this intimate connection, we fall back on our more primitive systems of defense—such as fight, flight, and/or freeze. (Porges, 2004)*

From conception, we resonate in tune or out of tune with those who bring us into this world (Schore, 1999). We look for who we are in the faces of our parents because to the small child, the parent is the whole world, God, judge, and jury. How they see us becomes how we see our- selves more than anyone cares to admit. Could we light up their faces simply by smiling at them or laughing or caressing their cheek? Did they respond to our little sad or anxious looks with comfort and interest? Could we feel their concern and their wish to relieve us of our worries? Or, did we feel dismissed or ridiculed, as if we were a burden or a disap- pointment? A combination of both? What was the quality of their touch? Did they make us feel seen or invisible?

Neuroception, a term coined by Stephen Porges (2004), former director of the Brain-Body Center at the University of Illinois at Chi- cago (2004), describes our innate ability to use intricate, meaning-laden, barely perceptible mind-body signals to establish bonds and commu- nicate our needs and intentions. While many of these communications are conscious, still more occur beneath the level of our awareness, as part of our animal self (Porges, 2004).

Neuroception is a system that has evolved over time to enable humans and mammals to establish the mutually nourishing bonds that we need to survive and thrive. It is also a built-in human security system that assesses, in the blink of an eye, whether or not the situations that we're encountering are safe or in some way threatening (Porges, 2004). According to Porges (2004), our *neuroception tells us if we can relax and be ourselves or if we need to self-protect.* If the signals that we're picking up from those we depend upon are indifferent, cold, dismissive, or threatening, that system sets off an inner alarm, which is followed by a cascade of mind-body responses, honed by eons of evolution to keep us from being harmed. Our body/mind sounds a distress signal, and that signal doesn't distinguish between the proverbial saber-toothed tiger or an angry or indifferent parent, older sibling, school bully, or spouse. *We brace for harm to our person on the inside as well as on the outside when those body/stress chemicals get triggered by fear. (Dayton, 2015)*

Because our capacity for self-regulation is developed within this co-state with our primary caregivers, we can be deeply hurt, frightened, or even traumatized when that co-state, or that parent/child connection, doesn't represent a secure attachment. A problematic co-state while growing up, might contribute to problems later in life.

The Subtle Disconnect

I was recently traveling to a conference when I encountered a scene in the restroom that has stayed with me. I was rushing along and glanced down at a baby who was in the middle of being changed by his mother. I first noticed his beautiful blond hair and blue eyes. But his eyes had something else—he had a vacant look. He looked very disconnected. I have, however, learned to question myself at these moments, and I thought, *Perhaps he's very tired; he is traveling, and probably this is his nap time. Maybe there is a developmental issue at play.* But he looked more than tired; he looked like he had given in or given up. *Such a little baby,* I thought, *Robust enough but so, so far away."* I let my gaze move up to his mother, and there it was. The mother was making no eye contact with the baby, no cooing, no little sounds, or reassuring touches in this very intimate and vulnerable moment from the point of view of the child. She, too, looked very far away. But even more, there she stood with huge, white earphones, the kind you'd use in a studio. She wasn't there, and her baby knew it. He *felt* it. When she did, for a brief moment, look at him, he lit up and connected immediately.

I see this in the park sometimes with caregivers. They are pushing a child along in the stroller, paying absolutely no attention to them. They are on the phone or simply disinterested, putting in the hours. Or, the child is wandering around, not knowing what to do, and they are receiving no help, care, or concern. No little moments of connection and guidance that would teach them the skills of playing and relating to other children.

It is these little moments that make a life. These barely perceptible interactions create a child who feels comfortable sustaining an intimate connection, a child who can learn, trust, and open his inner world to the inner world of another person.

When no one is "there" at the other end of the child's innocent attempts to connect, then learning how to be in comfortable, supportive, and authentic connection doesn't get developed and practiced in the thousand little ways that make a moment. In trauma-engendering interactions:

> People are not able to use their interactions to regulate their physiological states in relationship . . . *they are not getting anything back from the other person, that can help them to remain calm and regulated.* Quite the opposite, the other person's behavior is making them go into a scared, *braced-for-danger state. Their physiology is being up-regulated into a fight/ flight mode. (Porges)*

Our neuroseptic system is up-regulating and bracing for danger with the very people we wish to connect with or run to for a sense of safety. This is a subtle form of being traumatized that can be very hard to detect. A caregiver who is constantly critical and withholds cuddling and emotional support can feel traumatizing to the small child. A baby is born with and continues to feel a profound yearning and need for the parent's love and care. It is built into us as part of the survival of our species. Most parents feel a correspondingly overpowering longing to love and protect their children. But if the parent is overwhelmed by too many children and too little support, or if the circumstances of their lives are too wearing, they can resent the little ones in their charge or turn them over to people who do not love them or care well for them. They may be incapable of giving them the kind of thoughtful attention that will help them to build a solid sense of self. They can turn away when they should be turning toward. The child is not receiving the attuned responses from their caregiver that would help them absorb and internalize the skills of healthy connection. They are moon-walking, out on their own, not internalizing the skills of comfortable connection and not learning how to join in. If we want to understand why teenagers or young adults do violent and crazy things, or why students at school act out, we need to look at how children are being raised and cared for in their early years.

Faulty neuroception, Porges thinks, may underlie many of our relationship disorders. A failure to learn how to regulate our emotions and safe connection *within relationships* can impact how we live in relationships in the future.

So part of good parenting is to constantly soothe and restore the tiny moments of disconnection or rupture that are inevitable when a bond is this powerful. If there is a sense of disconnection and it is not followed by conscious cooing, calm, and reconnection, small children are left to make sense of the disconnection on their own. And they do so with very innocent, dependent, vulnerable, and childlike reasoning. Or, they develop shame around their needs or their desire to connect, then they disown parts of themselves around which they feel shame. Their "child-think" may go something like this:

- My parent doesn't care about my feelings;
- I'm safer alone, and I'm calmer if I disconnect;
- I am getting it wrong again;
- I'm not worth attention and love;

- Needing hurts, loving hurts, it's not worth it;
- I must be bad, or my needs are bad, or she/he wouldn't act like that.

Conversely the small child can internalize positive messages that become part of them:

- Everyone seems to like me;
- Anyone who gets to know me will like me;
- I am just good inside;
- I love being close; it feels so nice;
- The world is a friendly place;
- I am interesting and pleasing to others;
- I can find ways to meet my needs and wants.

One important thing to understand here is that even well-intended parents can cause significant emotional and psychological pain for their children. The child's limited brain development and their total dependency on their parent can make them very vulnerable to being hurt. And the opposite is equally true; simply loving and accepting your child will go a long way toward making them strong and resilient.

Picture a small child, innocent, just beginning to make sense of the world, a child whose primary world consists of immediate family and the few experiences that their parents connect them with. The child's size means that everything in their world seems very, very big. Their house is large. Other adults are huge. Their parents' heads seem to touch the ceiling or even the sky. Everything that happens in this little one's world has a forever kind of impact because the child has no sense of time really. The adults in their world are keepers of time, of circumstance, of food, love, a warm bed at night, and a roof over their heads. The child is both held in a mythical land of milk and honey and trapped in a world owned and run by someone else. If those someone elses are

benevolent and kind, the child learns that the world is a benevolent and kind place in which they can find love and safety. If the caregivers are selfish, neglectful, or abusive, the child learns that the world is a place that they cannot trust, a place in which they have to guard against constant threats to their sense of self.

Constantly gearing up to self-protect can lead to dysregulation in our limbic system. Stress chemicals are there for a reason: to prepare us for fight or flight. When we can do neither, when our size and dependence keep us in a situation that is causing us to brace for danger, we don't use up those stress chemicals, they stay inside of us and impact our health and well-being.

Trauma Can Be Subtle: Connection Versus Disconnection

"Trauma can occur any time that we encountered an experience that overwhelmed our capacity to cope with what's going on," says Daniel A. Seigel, MD, Executive Director of the Mindsight Institute. "So if we're an adult and we have trauma it's going to have one kind of impact. But if we're a young child and we experience trauma, especially in relationship to those we depend on, our caregivers, then the trauma takes on a different kind of impact. That kind of betrayal by our caregivers, leads to all kinds of ways where the developing brain for example, doesn't develop the kind of integrative circuits that it otherwise would. So developmental trauma, which means abuse, neglect or both early in life, has been shown to result in impairments in the growth of the fibers of the brain that take differentiated areas, like the left and the right or widely separated memory systems. The brain, in other words, compartmentalizes pain, and doesn't create a kind of relational coherence.

This kind of relational trauma continues to impact the way that we get along with people throughout our lives. When this type of pain dates from early childhood, it can be invisible to the naked eye, but it does not disappear. What we're left with are needs that we either don't even know we have or we don't know how to fill. This is not because our world or relationships won't let us but because we can't take in the caring and connection that would make us feel full. We keep self-protecting. We keep pushing away what we need because needing feels dangerous or because we're numb inside and cannot even feel our own yearning.

"The fundamental calamity," says Gabor Maté, author of *When the Body Says No*, "was not that you were sexually abused, was not that you were beaten, was not that you were abandoned, was not that your parents couldn't love you in the way you needed to be loved, it's that as a result of all that, *you lost the connection to yourself. That's the trauma; it's what's happening internally.* Had it not resulted in the disconnection with yourself, you would not have been traumatized. And so what are we looking for then? It's that reconnection with ourselves. Why? Because if it's so painful to be myself, I'd better disconnect. If it's so painful for me to be aware of my gut feelings and to be able to assert them and to manifest them and declare them, I'd better disconnect from my gut feelings. And it's that disconnection with the gut feelings that happens right in the body, that's the trauma."

Recently, I witnessed an interaction between a little five-year-old boy and his parents. The child was clearly frightened by a family interaction in which he was disciplined. He was crying hard and trying to defend himself. I reassured him that he had done nothing all that wrong and that even if he had, it was okay. I told him I made mistakes all day long. He then relaxed enough to talk a little, but was still pretty distressed. When I asked him to tell me how he was feeling, he said something that I will never forget. "I feel like I am in tiny little pieces scattered all over the room, and I can't pull them together enough to think of a word to tell you."

I was dumfounded at what this five-year-old was able to understand and articulate. Perhaps because he had not learned yet to lie, perhaps because he was normally happy in his relationship with his parents, or perhaps because his parents' faces were so caring and concerned, he could just feel enough to identify that he couldn't really feel. He didn't need to shut down to self-protect. Once he put this into words, it was sort of miraculous to watch him. He went from looking tense and white to having color again. He then found a few words to describe how scared he was, when his parents suddenly turned around, with angry and accusing looks. He went back over the whole interaction and "told the story."

When I interrupted with a well-meaning question, he said, "No, I want to tell the whole thing first, from the beginning." His mother signaled that he likes to do this, to tell the story from the beginning, and she sweetly and sensitively respected his wish. After just a few minutes, he had put the full experience into order. He'd brought all the parts together into one whole, integrated description of what happened. He created a narrative, *with himself back in it,* no longer frozen and looking from the outside in, but alive again on the inside, owning his own experience. Because caring adults helped him to ground, to come back into his body, to feel and put his inner experience into words, he felt seen and listened to. For a moment he couldn't see himself, but we sat together, we kept seeing him until he could come back. We invited him to take a breath and tell us what was going on inside of him. He could, and he did. And once he had told his little trauma story, he slipped off of the couch and went back to carefree playing. *He let it go.*

The amazing thing about this, was that it mirrored so perfectly the research on trauma. It was a little, living case study of the psychic splintering that can be part of feeling deeply frightened. And it illustrated the natural need we have to tell the trauma story, to give it a beginning, a middle, and an end so that it can organically fall back within the context of our morning, of our day, of our lives. This little five-year-old had never read the trauma literature; he just did it naturally.

But when there is no caring adult with enough bandwidth to do this for and with a hurting child or to even notice that they are hurting, then the child is left to hold this feeling of frozenness and scatteredness all alone. Or maybe they are told not to feel it, that nothing bad happened or that they are the problem. And then these experiences that could be small accumulate, they get sticky and become psychically glued to each other and they live inside of the developing self in a hidden and humiliated silence.

Mending the Breech

There are many small breeches in connection throughout the day, but a good-enough parent will help the child to mend them and restore connection and a sense of pleasure and safety. When these breeches remain unrepaired by the parent/child relationship, they appear again and again throughout life. The narcissist who cannot reverse roles in their mind with another person and empathize with someone outside of their own orbit because they still remain locked in their own, may be living out this childhood trauma of disconnection. The borderline personality who jumps in and out of a sense of intimate relatedness one moment, then if sensing rejection in any form becomes devaluing of or hostile to another person the next, may be oscillating back and forth between clinging to and pushing away the closeness and connection that they crave with another person.

> Trauma impels people both to withdraw from close relationships and to seek them desperately.... The profound disruption in basic trust, the common feelings of shame, guilt and inferiority and the need to avoid reminders of the trauma that might be found in social life, all foster withdrawal from close relationships. But the terror of the traumatized infant intensifies the need for protective attachments therefore the traumatized person frequently alternates between isolation and anxious clinging to others. (Herman, 1997)

Much mental illness circulates around these early dynamics, these failures of love and closeness that were not adequately repaired. The traumatized or hurt child needs to be soothed and brought back into a state of comfortable connection. When this doesn't happen, they do not have enough actual experience of mending and repairing moments of disconnection to take with them into their own intimate relationships later in life.

The Two-Minute Tune In

Dr. Bruce Perry talks about the importance of using "relation contagion" to repair the endless relational breeches that are part of life. "Your history of connectedness is more powerful than your history of adversity. Present connection is able to buffer present stressors and create an environment for healing for past trauma." He encourages us to "create therapeutic moments. Hundreds of five second moments, provided mostly by parents, teachers and friends," Perry feels can change the course of a life and should be the way, or at least a way that we conceptualize healing. "Being fully present for two minutes...it's a powerful thing to do, these moments last and last."

Attachment and Love

Ask yourself these questions and write whatever comes to mind.

1. How did I experience the arms, gaze and connection of my mother, father and other primary caregivers (animals may also have been experienced as primary attachment figures). Write their names and whatever words or phrases that come to mind.

_____

_____

_____

_____

_____

2. How am I recreating these styles of relating in my intimate relationships today?

_____

_____

_____

_____

_____

3. Which styles are working for me, which ones seem enhancing to my close relationships?

_____

_____

_____

_____

_____

4. Which styles are undermining closeness? Which styles create conflict and mis-understanding?

_____

_____

_____

_____

5. If I could say one thing to my mother or father it would be . . .

_____

_____

_____

_____

6. If I could say one thing to my "inner child" or the kid I was from where I stand today it would be . . .

_____

_____

_____

_____

7. What do I wish my parents had done differently?

_____

_____

_____

_____

8. What am I glad my parents did just the way they did it?

_____

_____

_____

_____

CHAPTER SIX

Codependency: An Anxious Attachment

"The greatest hazard of all, losing one's self,
can occur very quietly in the world, as if it were nothing at all.
No other loss can occur so quietly; any other loss—an arm,
a leg, five dollars, a wife, etc.—is sure to be noticed."

—Søren Kierkegaard,
*The Sickness Unto Death: A Christian Psychological
Exposition for Upbuilding and Awakening*

Perhaps at the very root of codependency is a wish to have the parent and family we need, glad to have us around, to be able to put a smile on their faces when they turn in our direction, to avoid a dark look that we fear might be leveled against us. It's an attempt to stay safe. When this natural urge to please and connect becomes fraught with anxiety and confusion, as can happen in families where there is addiction, abuse or neglect, relational connections both with ourselves and those close to us can become distorted. One of the ways that this can manifest is in what we call codependency.

We can have a codependent connection even with ourselves that can feel conditional and tenuous. We have trouble with personal boundaries, we don't know where we leave off and another person begins. We lack the skills to tune in calmly to what is going on inside of us and we don't necessarily feel that we have the right to our own feelings or our own experience. And we don't know how to attend to our own needs, rather they get mixed up with what we think are the needs of others.

We can have a codependent connection with others in which we're more occupied with what might be going on in their minds, than in our own. We're outwardly focused, we scan for potential problems and see need and want in others whether or not it is there because we can't see our own. We often feel overly responsible for the feelings of others or guilty when we want to take care of ourselves. In understanding the depth and breadth of codependency, it might be useful to find out where the word began, it's etymology.

Initially the word codependency grew out of the twelve-step term *co-addict*, or *co-dependent*. It was a kind of grassroots way of naming the situation that a spouse found themselves in when they were connected in every way possible to an addict: married to them, having children with them, and living their daily lives or trying to live them together.

Now picture the 1980s, when the word somehow went viral (even without an internet) and people were streaming into conferences and twelve-step rooms or buying books on codependency because they had a sense that they, too, identified. They were seeing themselves in the kinds of symptomatology and family dynamics that surround addiction. So codependency is a term whose meaning has grown with those who use it. It has come to refer to a constellation of behaviors designed to *accommodate someone else*. And it manifests as interpersonal fusion, blurred boundaries, and anxiety around deep connection (whether or not an addict is even in the picture).

Codependency is often conceptualized as a set of placating, behaviors. "I was being so codependent last night, I just kept giving myself away." Or "I'm codependent with my daughter; I can't set boundaries." However, seeing codependency in this way tends to make us think that changing our behaviors vis a vis that other person, is the entire solution to becoming less codependent. But this, of course, means that change is still *focused on another person.*

Once we decide we're codependent, (or worse, once a therapist tells us we are), we may think that pulling away from the natural and caring behaviors that accompany connection and intimacy and constructing a slalom course of boundaries that virtually no one can navigate, is the solution. We overcorrect. We go from one extreme to the other, from overly accommodating to controlling and rigid. We think if we construct "firm" boundaries we'll feel less shaky inside. But as often as not, we're erecting those boundaries as a way to manage our own unconscious anxiety. And when we can't look at our own anxiety and wonder what might be driving it, we leave the biggest part of the solution to our problems, out. Namely us.

Codependency grows out of a normal, biological desire to adapt our own behavior to fit into the group. We are pack animals, and we naturally want to vibrate in tune with those around us. But when those around us cannot attune themselves to us, when they cannot be pleased or when our primary caregiver's mood rules the environment, then what's a kid to do?

Codependency can begin very, very early as a form of nervousness that our overpowering need to attach to our primary caregivers will not necessarily be met with an equally powerful urge to connect with us. We come to be anxious about just *how* to connect with our primary caregivers, to get what we want, to feel accepted and valued. If, as children, when we look into our parent's face for reassurance and love, we find rejection and disinterest, we can worry that the world will feel that same way about us because for the small child our parents are the world. They are the gatekeepers of life and all it holds.

So codependents spend a lot of time managing the world around them so that they can feel less anxious. And here it all begins.

One of my own manifestations of codependency is over-functioning. If I am part of any group that I want to continue to be a part of
I tend to over-function, I do too much or more than is called for. I
try to anticipate the needs of others without them having to ask, not
consciously really, I just catch myself at it usually well after I have been
doing it for a while. My family fell apart while I was still young. I was
in my early teens when it went from six people to two, and it eventually
became just Mom and me with my father in another state. My mother
was fairly spent by this point and had little energy to give motherhood
or anything else. And besides, she had clearly decided that her family
had ended and she had given up on trying to create any semblance of
one. I found that the best way to really stay in a positive place with her,
was to need very little for myself and to take care of her, to try to keep
her in a positive frame of mind (again, a real challenge). My father was
still drinking and though we were very much in touch, he was far away.
So I got a job, saved money and put my mother's needs first. I did this
with such gusto that I lost track of what mine were. Maybe it even got
my mind off of my own grief to look after her, caretaking behavior can
be a manifestation of our own, unconscious grief. Whatever led to my
doing it, it's what I did. The upside was that I felt a tremendous sense of
empowerment at being able to take actions to solve my own problems.
(And hers). Or so I thought. What I didn't understand at the time was
that I was over-functioning for my mother's under-functioning and
to fill in the desperate sense of emptiness that surrounded us both. I
stopped having overnights because I didn't want to leave my mother
alone and I bought her presents to make her feel better. I included her in
my time with my friends. When she didn't want to take me to the doctor
to get a clear health report for the swim team, I dropped the swim team.
I thought of her all the time. I did the cooking if there was any. I tried
to ask for nothing and I think I pretty much succeeded at that.

However, the buffering elements in my life were excellent. I was very close to my grandmother and aunt and uncle, I was also close to church and I had a lovely school and friends all around me. And my family had actually been wonderful in all sorts of ways until my parents came up against more than they could handle. Eventually, my mother remarried and she had what she always called "another fine husband," and we had a really wonderful stepfather who came to regard us as "his kids, too," as he said. I always admired that my mom never spoke badly of our father, nor did my father speak badly of her. They recognized, in their Greek way, that this would be damaging to us and, besides, they knew that they had built a family with their best intentions. When Mom married Walt, my father called to congratulate him and to tell him that he was marrying "a wonderful woman." And Walt always admired that. All of my parents were capable of being big people.

It was in creating my own family that the part of me who longed for a harmonious family came alive again and started to feel. I felt both the pain of my earlier loss and the healing of having another chance to create a safe home. Even though I couldn't get back what I lost as a kid, I got the help I needed so that I didn't sabotage my ability to create a good home for my own children, to regain that beautiful sense of trust and belonging. Without recovery I don't think my husband and I would have been able to do as well as we have, we threw ourselves into everything we could try. We sincerely wanted to find our way out of the kind of pain that just keeps recreating itself without help or intervention. We knew we didn't have the answers and were open to listening to others who might know more. And they did. And now we do. Our happy lives we both feel have been a great gift of recovery.

Trauma, Hypervigilance, and Codependency

From the trauma perspective, codependency is a form of hypervigilance based on feeling anxious around deep, relational connection.

"When we get scared, our left brain, the language part of the brain, becomes overwhelmed and shuts down...What remains very active, however, is the emotional scanning system in our right brain. The part of our brain that scans and remains hypervigilant is, in fact, working overtime when we are scared—codependency in the making. Children who regularly experience relationship trauma often learn that they can fend off trouble if they can stay hyper-focused on reading the other person's emotional signals." (van der Kolk 1997) They can become very adept at reading other people's moods, often to the exclusion of their own. They become habitually outer-focused and may lose touch with what is going on inside of them.

How Trauma Affects Our Sense-of-Self

The self is a rather abstract concept. Although we think of it as stable and fixed, it is really a set of ideas that is fluid and always under construction. It's a *sense of self* and we build it in relation to others. When we construct our sense of self within a family that is reasonably stable and feels supportive, a family that lets us say what is on our minds and in our hearts and who thinks well of us, who we feel seen and understood by, we have a pretty good chance of growing up with a solidly constructed sense of self. A sense of self that is secure enough to feel coherent and integrated and porous enough to continue to take in and incorporate new learning. A self that can adjust to new situations without abandoning its ephemeral core or source or consciousness of wholeness. When this is not the case, when saying what is on our minds and hearts leads to pain, rejection, or criticism and we internalize too many negative messages, or when we get the message that we're dear to someone as long as we play by their rules and consider their needs before our own, we may become afraid to take up space. Afraid that if we are ourselves, are too needy or have conflicting opinions and desires with those we love, people just won't like us. The result of this can be a disconnection with our authentic self in favor of developing a self that is pleasing to those from whom we're seeking acceptance. If the tacit or overt demand from the family is that we be who it needs or wants us to be rather than ourselves, we may create a false self in order to feel accepted.

We become used to hiding certain parts of who we are, we run through a mental checklist of what we can allow to show and what we need to hold back. As a result of this, our ability to be ourselves with others becomes hamstrung or limited. We begin to create a self that will please others or maybe get them off our backs, a self that doesn't ask us to come in touch with the fear of rejection or inner pain we carry, we create what psychologists refer to as a *false self.*

The phenomenon of false self-functioning is often seen in alcoholic families or other types of families that have impossible standards of who and what to be, such as with some, but certainly not all wealthy, rigidly religious, political, or military families. It is also associated with pain-filled, dysfunctional families. When there is fear in the family, as is often the case with addiction, operating from a false self can feel safer than being vulnerable and real. Staying safe and "looking good" become of paramount importance. The family can collude in this type of functioning and opt for being a "looking good" family who presents a together perfect image to the world that can become rather air tight, it's designed not to reveal the anxiety they carry unconsciously. To this end, children and even adults become what will please and protect the system rather than who they really feel like on the inside. And eventually they are out of touch with their insides.

Caring for Our Disowned Parts

When someone who has become dependent on false self-functioning goes into therapy or enters a twelve-step program, they can go through a period of feeling very vulnerable and shaky, because they are removing their coping strategy and exposing the pain underneath it. But over time, new emotional habits get created, and new ways of healthy coping get practiced and adopted. This person can become much more comfortable "living in their own skin."

Really healing from codependency or PTSD issues is a gradual rebuilding of our own sense of self within in the context of relationships. It is learning to stay connected to ourselves *while* in the presence of and connected to another person and allowing that person to stay connected to themselves, as well.

We can learn how to care for our own, perhaps disowned inner parts. Richard Schwartz, creator of Internal Family Systems Therapy (IFS) says, "There's an essence within people that already has the qualities of a good attachment figure and can become a good parent to wounded inner parts. Rather than just watch our thoughts and emotions parade by, we see these as emanating from suffering beings, and we can use compassion to get to know them."

The more we can strengthen our own inner world by witnessing its inner workings and paying attention to self-care and self-awareness, the more buffered we'll be when it comes to dealing with the forces around us.

Self-Monitoring

How do we check in with ourselves when we're worried that we're losing our footing? Try asking yourself a couple of questions when you find yourself tangled up in codependent behaviors:

1. *Am I scared?* Maybe even triggered? Am I seeing the other person as the problem and fixing them as the solution to the problem? Do I need to sit with this feeling *I am having*?
2. *What is getting triggered inside of me?* Am I layering an old attachment fear onto this new relationship? Am I bracing for

danger because of what the feelings of intimacy and dependence are triggering in me from my past experiences with closeness and connection?

3. *Am I self-medicating and actually weakening my positive connection with myself?* Am I using processes or substances to manage my moods because I am not successfully managing them on my own?

4. *What can I do to strengthen my connection with myself right now?* Am I feeling overwhelmed and do I just need to take some personal space for a while so that things can come clear or so that I can un-hook and have some ME time? Am I ignoring self-care and do I need to pay attention to exercise, nutrition, relaxation, meditation? Do I need to UN-PLUG, limit my news/social media time?

Once you learn to tune in on yourself when you're having a "codependent slip," you can figure out what is going on that is making you want to control, fix or placate.

Write a Letter to Your
Adult Self from Your Inner Child

What does the child inside of you want from your adult self when in a triggered state?

Dear _____, *(Use the name or nickname you were called as a child)*

_____

_____

_____

_____

_____

_____

_____

_____

_____

_____

_____

_____

_____

_____

_____

_____

_____

_____

_____

_____

(put closing here)

Your name _____

Write a Letter to Your Inner Child

From your adult self, knowing what you know today:

Dear _____, *(Use the name or nickname you were called as a child)*

_____

_____

_____

_____

_____

_____

_____

_____

_____

_____

_____

_____

_____

_____

_____

_____

_____

(put closing here)

Your name _____

CHAPTER SEVEN

Walking on Eggshells: Living Inside an Addicted Family System

Most people are only as needy
as their unmet needs.

—Amir Levine *Attached*

There are lots of ways that people describe the experience of living with addiction: *Walking on eggshells, never knowing which end is up, waiting for the other shoe to drop, see-saw, roller coaster, topsy-turvy, black and white.* Initially, these are the dynamics surrounding the addict. Eventually, they are the dynamics of the family as a whole. The intra-*personal* becomes the *inter-personal* as family members absorb and mirror the thinking, feeling and behavior that surround addiction until eventually, everyone in the family starts to act a little drunk.

Without sufficient buffering experiences from extended family and community, children in this family can start to feel misunderstood and misread, they don't know where to go to find "normal." There is a loss of self-regulation and relational regulation. When this is the case, then these dysfunctional relational dynamics that are part of the family environment, pass through another generation. The children act out.

87

Developing a working understanding of some of the common relational dynamics that are part of dysfunction can make them easier to identify and move through. Knowing that they are not all that unusual normalizes them and allows a family to achieve some emotional and psychological distance as they work through old pain and adopt and build new and more resilient strategies for getting along.

Context Organizes Us:
The Influence of the Family

Salvador Minuchin was a pioneer of treating the family system as a whole rather than treating the individual alone. Initially, Minuchin and his cohorts were looking at ways to transform the institutional settings in which delinquents lived, in order to help them to get better.

Minuchin's team discovered however, that their attempts to treat only the acting-out child, did not seem to work unless and until they somehow got more family members involved. "So our desire to do family therapy," recounts Minuchin, "sprang from an understanding that what we were doing wasn't working" (interview, *Family Networker* video). This awareness is what evolved into what we now know to be family therapy. Minuchin viewed mental health problems in the child as arising from the family system in which they grew up. His focus was to change the system in order to help the child. He follows a few basic principles in his approach:

- *Context organizes us.* Our behaviors grow out of the system in which we were raised. To change the behaviors of a young person, we need to change the system. To understand ourselves, we need to understand our system.
- The family is the primary context, for developing our "matrix of identity."

- The family's structure consists of recurrent patterns of interaction that its members develop over time, as they accommodate each other.
- A well-functioning family is *not defined by the absence of stress or conflicts, but by how effectively it handles them,* as it responds to the developing needs of its members and the changing conditions in its environment.
- The job of Minuchin's strength based structural family (SFT) therapist is to find and mobilize underutilized strengths. In utilizing strengths, the family is able to marshal its competencies in order to fight the disease. They can then spontaneously come up with healthier strategies for managing challenges and fostering resilience and strength. Hopefully, this will also improve interactions so that they become less antagonistic and more collaborative.

Nathan Ackerman, another pioneer of marriage and family therapy, saw family issues as emerging when family members no longer worked together in complementary ways. For example, he saw the scapegoat or *symptom bearing child* as potentially wearing or acting out pain and/or anger between the parents or family members that wasn't being looked at and dealt with. We see this phenomenon in families where one or both parents are addicts and in denial, in these cases kids internalize the unspoken family hurt and desperation and they exhibit behaviors that look troubled. Then the parents suddenly pull together to "help" the child who a school might have identified as having problems. It is an insidious epigenetic manifestation of untreated family addiction and dysfunction in which the pain of living with dysfunction and/or addiction evidences itself in a child being anxious or depressed or somehow not thriving. Eventually this anxious/depressed child may reach for drugs and alcohol and addiction rolls through another generation.

Healthy families evolve, they grow into new constellations, and can foster both intimacy and autonomy. The roles in a healthy family are flexible enough so that people can share responsibilities and in place enough so that each person lives up to the demands of their own role. There is empathy for the position of each role, for example, a mother is empathized with for the unique pressures of her role and a father is for the pressures and responsibilities that he undertakes. And children's roles are empathized with too, the youngest is allowed to be young and given a certain protection, the oldest is recognized for both the sacrifices and privileges of being the oldest. Those children in between can be seen in their own light with both the difficulties they deal with and the contributions that they make. The family as a whole can pull together when needed to do anything from making a grocery run to getting through tough times, they can work together as a system and their ability to empathize with each other's positions is a source of resilience and strength.

But families that have incorporated the profoundly debilitating dynamics surrounding addiction, that have learned to hide and deny problems, and that have stopped talking to each other about what really matters, can develop a habit of shutting each other out by withdrawing from genuine connections. Their interactions become forced or fake. Trauma makes us hold rigidly to our own point of view, we're afraid to see the other person's side of things because it feels threatening to our being able to hold onto ours. We're not good at hanging onto a sense of our own self while giving some ground. In families where there is trauma, roles aren't necessarily respected and maintained or they are maintained so rigidly that there is no flexibility. Also, when people get hurt and are never allowed to make their hurt feelings known in a safe way, they continue to feel misunderstood or they become self-righteous, judgmental and opinionated. Then there is even less healthy communication and understanding so mistrust grows and family members pull back into their own, segregated worlds. They may feel safe, sharing genuinely with one person but not others, so they form factions. Then some family members feel left out, which only deepens the divides.

As a family continues not to talk openly about the problems it is experiencing but relies instead on covert alliances and triangulation to communicate meaningful feelings and thoughts, information becomes siloed. And problems set in. Sometimes their deeper defenses such as denial, both as individuals and as a system, are just too embedded to be able to envision and embrace change.

Ackerman identified that if "the conflict between family members became chronic, the family was at risk for re-organization into competing factions." In this case the family is no longer functioning as one system, but as competing or disconnected factions. These factions may present themselves as pairs, clusters, and subsystems between and among family members within the overall group. These affiliations may have begun in pursuit of safety and homeostasis. However, as a family grows progressively more scared and secretive, these pairs and clusters can become discreet coalitions that are increasingly rigid and covert. "Change and growth within the system, become constricted. Roles become rigid, narrowly defined, or stereotyped—or shift rapidly, causing confusion.

Communication which is core to change and growth, becomes very difficult because clusters and factions have formed, and they compete for power. If any family member tries to defy this way of operating rather than join a faction, they may get marginalized or pointed to as the problem. So family members may fight, one-up each other, seek power through alignment with a parent, or break up into sibling or sibling–parent factions. And they do not develop good skills of self-reflection and negotiation. Factions can become increasingly estranged from each other, which may result in distance and splintering. "For a family's behavior to be stable, flexibility and adaptability of roles are essential. Roles within the family, which change over time, must allow for maturing children to gain an appropriate degree of autonomy."

Dysfunctional Family Dynamics

We learn not to trust our guts in dysfunctional families. We don't check things out. We may no longer read signals correctly. We get disconnected from our emotions, from our inner guidance system. So to cope with this, family members come up with strategies to stay safe and to hang onto a sense of balance, albeit a dysfunctional one. They develop styles of relating that are designed to keep them from feeling like the ground beneath them is giving way. Family systems therapy has identified several relating styles that can develop in dysfunctional family systems.

Some of them are:

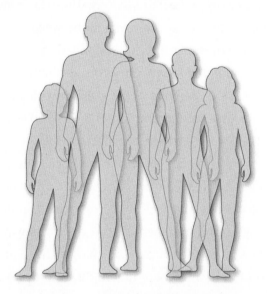

Enmeshment

Enmeshment: Family members who are struggling to feel safe can develop enmeshed styles of relating. They may become *overly* close or *overly* concerned, and *overly* involved with each other in a way that interferes with autonomy. It can be difficult to maintain healthy boundaries in an enmeshed family. The idea is to agree, and disagreement can be seen as disloyal, aggressive, or bad.

Enmeshment can be a family style of relating that can be learned and passed along from previous generations, or it can be the result of living with relational trauma.

Enmeshed styles can also be the manifestation of leaky and less than conscious feelings. For example, if our anxiety gets triggered by something and we aren't able to own it as our own feeling and right-size it within ourselves, we may *project* it outwards, we make it about some-one else: "Are you okay?" Somehow this feels more palatable to us than asking ourselves the question: "What's going on with *me*?" Not being able to distinguish our feelings from someone else's can characterize enmeshment and of course codependency. On the flip side, being able to make our own decisions while at the same time being aware of their impact on others can be a sign of non-enmeshment.

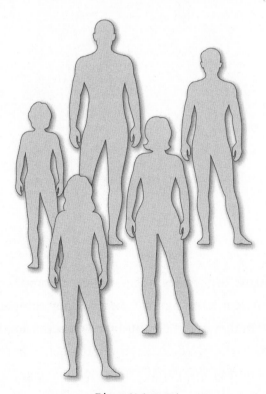

Disengagement

Disengagement: Disengagement is the flip side of enmeshment. Unable to gain a sense of healthy separateness or space, family members vault to the opposite pole and disengage to gain relief. Disengaged family members function separately and autonomously in their day-to-day living. Their boundaries can be rigid, and they feel isolated and/or disconnected from each other. Addicted family systems sometimes cycle between these two styles. They are enmeshed in their basic mode of operating, but because they aren't good at having normal, healthy boundaries, when they start to feel claustrophobic, they create conflict in order to gain space, and then they disengage.

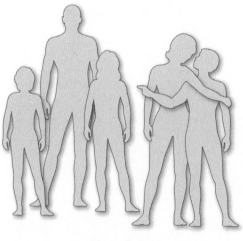

Triangulation

Triangulation: In families without open communication, people do not talk directly with each other. Rather, when someone has a complaint or concern, they say it to a third party: they triangulate. They do not talk directly to the person with whom they have an issue; they *talk about that person* to a third party. Triangulation creates fissures within the family. And the children in the family can mimic this aligning with each other, to gain power over the other children, for example, two siblings align against a third sibling. In families that become increasingly dysfunctional, these alignments can become long term and permanent, part of the family fractures.

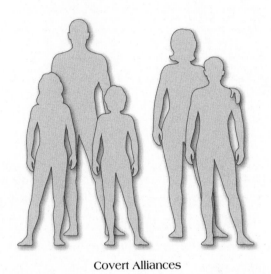

Covert Alliances

Covert Alliances: A covert alliance is a sort of unspoken, even clandestine power agreement. It's an attempt to consolidate a sense of place and/or control within the system. Covert alliances can create power dyads or clusters for some, while excluding and disempowering others. With covert alliances information becomes siloed, some family members are in the know while others are left out and this is a breeding ground for envy and sibling competition.

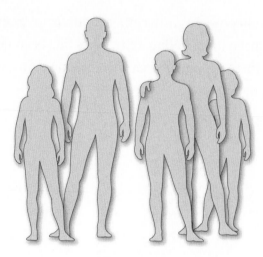

Silent Partner

Silent Partner: When partners are not functioning well as a team, when they cannot talk over and take responsibility for their own issues and problems, they may each pull a child close to them and turn them into their little partner. This child's job is to be loyal to their parent. As the parent's "silent partner," they can have a kind of de facto power over their parents and over their siblings. But they are caught in a serious loyalty bind between their two parents, and they are being used by those parents, often at the expense of their own comfortable development. This also creates sibling competition that the children suffer for, but the parents are responsible for. The relationship can be sexualized, but this is not necessarily so. More often, the child fills in for intimacy and companionship and for shoring up a parent who feels insecure or unsupported.

Trauma Bonding: Trauma bonds usually occur in relationships involving inconsistent reinforcement or cycles of promises and rewards alternating with some form of punishment (emotional, psychological or physical). Families where there are addicts, abusive/neglectful parents,

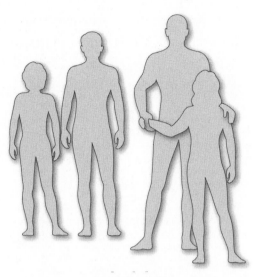

Trauma Bonding

or some form of violence or bullying tend to be environments where trauma bonds get set up. Trauma bonds gain traction when there is intensity, complexity, manipulation, chaos, and/or inconsistency. Patrick Carnes who developed the term, writes in his book, *Betrayal Bonds,* "Abandonment and trauma are at the core of addictions." This refers to addictions of all sorts: alcohol, drugs, sex, gambling, work, cyber and perhaps food as well.

Trauma bonds recreate themselves in relationships whether or not there are drugs and alcohol and can pass down through the generations. We may have trouble disengaging from those with whom we have developed trauma bonds regardless of the regular fighting and the consistent nonperformance. We feel helpless to change them and stuck in a pattern that we can't see our way out of. We are loyal to the hope or promise that something might change and the ever-present feeling (or threat) that we need this person in order to feel whole. Or we may be stuck in trying to fulfill someone else's idea of who we should be, even though they themselves may fall far short of the standards they set for us.

I would speculate that we can and are developing types of trauma bonds with news and social media in which we're afraid of what we might feel in relation to them, they agitate our inner world and hold us hostage to fear, anxiety and/or trying to live up to unrealistic expectations.

Abuser versus Victim Dynamics

Abuser-vs-Victim Dynamics: In alcoholic or dysfunctional families, there is always a time when things seem to be "normal," and we keep trying to get back to that feeling.

One of the relational patterns that can grow out of this feeling of hope versus disappointment is the abuser-versus-victim dynamic. We might see this dynamic as a manifestation of trauma bonding. It is part of the abuser's tactic to alternate between a super intimacy, "love bombing," and then accusations and devaluation. The victim then wonders what they have done to alienate the wonderful side of the abuser, and they obsess about getting them back. The victim feels as if they are getting something very wrong, that they need to make up for. The abuser remains firm in their blame, accusation, and devaluation.

Parentified Child

Parentified Child: As the parents relinquish responsibilities for caring for their own kids, those responsibilities get picked up by their other children. Siblings raise siblings, they become little parents. This can work if the parents are still acting like parents and the children feel their parents' mature and caring love, if it is a conscious, valued and appreciated filling in. But when parents barely have enough time and energy to make it through the day, when they feel anxious, stressed, and just vacate the responsibilities of their parental roles, siblings raising siblings can be a breading ground for problems. Along with being loving and fun, older children may resent caring for younger ones and missing out on their own activities. And if they do not feel appreciated by their parent, they may look to the younger child as a source of affection, appreciation, and even obeisance. They may want a kind of authority over younger siblings or a loyalty that isn't healthy for either of them. They may bully or take their sense of lack out on someone younger or more defenseless.

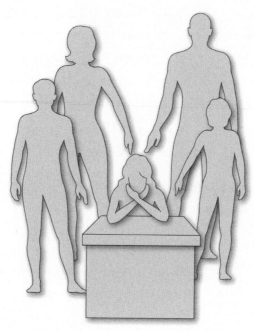

Symptom Bearing Child/Scapegoat

Symptom-Bearing Child/Scapegoat When there is trouble in the parent relationship that isn't being dealt with in mature ways, one child can become symptomatic on behalf of the couple or the family. This symptom-bearing child can also be referred to as the "identified patient" or the "scapegoat." This is the kid who becomes the problem to somehow take the attention off of the sinking ship. Maybe they act out, fail, underperform or get into trouble. There can also be a powerful secondary gain for the parents and even family members in having a "problem" to focus on. Warring parents can pull together in an effort to "help" the child who looks to be in the most trouble, which has the effect of taking the focus off of their own problems. Parents can feel effective, concerned, or worried about one of their children and set about fixing that child, what they should be fixing within their own relationship. This role can also have high value to the siblings who may experience relief in letting one sibling "wear" the family pain or problem identity which can lift that identity off of them. Siblings can feel both validated because what the scapegoat or "symptom-bearing" child is acting out is in them as well, but also—and this is the insidious part—they can now safely disown their own pain and pin it on the person manifesting it. Welcome to Dysfunctional Family Dynamics 101.

SOCIAL ATOM

Instructions: Complete in the space provided on the page after the sample, under the heading "Your Social Atom." Using circles to represent females and triangles to represent males (use a broken line if you include someone deceased) and squares for institutions, first locate yourself in any size and location on the page that feels right. Next, locate significant people (or pets) in whatever size or distance in relationship to you that feels right. The social atom can represent a particular time period, a particular moment or can just be a general snapshot of your family of origin. Your social atom can also include anyone who you felt was significant in your network, be it an aunt, uncle, neighbor, priest, rabbi or family friend. The genogram grew out of the social atom. But the social atom is a more flexible and diagnostic instrument. It can reflect the nature of relationships and it can include any and all significant relationships. This makes it particularly suitable for today's less traditional families.

SAMPLE

Social Atom Narrative: "Mom and my sister are overlapped, they act like clones of each other and my brother hangs in there, too. My other sister is floating out there sort of on her own. I am next to dad and my dogs. Grammie is great; so are my aunt and uncle. I like school and church. I play with my neighbor a lot, too."

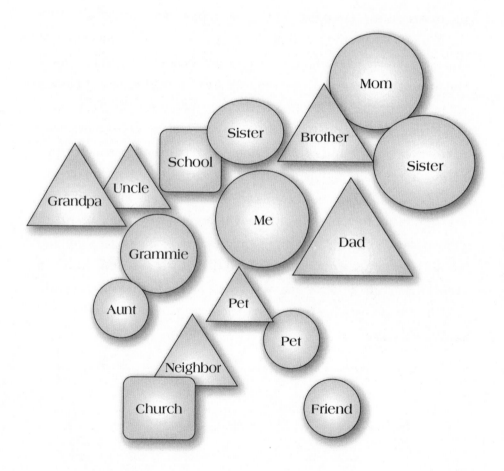

Your Social Atom

Questions to go with your social atom:

1. Write a short narrative describing your social atom.

_____

_____

_____

_____

2. Who do you feel close to? Describe.

_____

_____

_____

_____

3. Who do you feel distant from? Describe.

_____

_____

_____

_____

4. Who do you feel anxious around or tension with? Describe.

_____

_____

_____

_____

5. Is anyone enmeshed? If so, who, and describe.

_____

_____

_____

_____

6. Are their covert alliances or clusters? If so who, describe.

_____

_____

_____

_____

7. Are some of you trauma-bonded? If so who, describe.

_____

_____

_____

_____

8. Is there triangulation? Do you talk directly to each other or about each other?

_____

_____

_____

_____

9. Is there a symptom-bearing child? If so, who?

_____

_____

_____

_____

10. Is there a "little parent"? If so, who, please describe.

_____

_____

_____

_____

11. Are any of the children silent partners of the parents? If so, who, please describe.

12. If you could say something as the child in this particular family to your grown up self, what would it be?

13. If you were to say something to yourself within this social atom from outside of it, from a more mature and distanced place, what would you say?

CHAPTER EIGHT

Siblings: Passing Down the Pain

Someone I loved once gave me a box full of darkness.
It took me years to understand
that this, too, was a gift.

—Mary Oliver

We would have family meetings, randomly called by my father, often when he'd have had too much to drink or was sort of hung over (not that I knew that then). At this particular gathering, he was droning on and on about how family always had to stick together. Always. No matter what.

Maybe I wasn't the only one whose attention was wandering. Maybe that's why he resorted to visual aids. Mom looked dazed. The rest of us, I think, were trying to seem interested enough, so he'd stop talking sooner. *Not that I would ever know what was going on in their minds.* One thing I did know, though, we'd never talk about it.

Anyway, Dad wanted some pencils to illustrate his point and, as a Virgo, Mom was always a believer in sharpened pencils with eraser tips put on the top of them. She had them at the ready and broke her zoned-out expression long enough to hand them over in their orange paisley papier mâché holder.

"You see these pencils? You see them?" asked Dad in his Greek accent.

We nodded. (We see them; we see them.)

"Count them, one, two thhhrrreee, fooor, fife, seex."

(We're counting; we're counting.)

"Iff I hholdt them all togetherr, they arre strongggk. You see even I cannot break them" (like he was Hercules or something). He feigned tugging at them, doing his best to break them without success (six yellow bits of wood strained at his pencil prowess).

"But if I hhholdt jest one, look what hheppens,"

At this point, Dad broke that one, poor, pathetic, yellow, sharpened pencil with the pretty eraser, and it made a snapping noise that I think I can still hear on a quiet night.

It was a stunning and lasting lesson.

All I knew for sure, my take away at the tender age of six, was that I really, *really* didn't want to ever, under any circumstances, be that one pencil that popped in two splintered, wretched, raw, and exposed edges. (I do remember thinking that if I could keep the half with the eraser and just sort of sharpen it... but I quickly blotted that out of my mind as disloyal and stupid).

There was only one conclusion to draw from the pencil lesson. Stick together. Family first, family forever, family no matter what.

All children go through stages of attachment and individuation, negotiating everything from who gets the extra cookie to who gets which identity. It's a natural and healthy part of growing up. But in the addicted family system where time, energy and love are all overtaxed, and chaos, competition, and heartache are baked into the system, sibling complications can become overwhelming. When children become parentified and raise each other or when parents pull them in as surrogate confidants or partners, things get strained. A parent, if they are healthy at all, wants their child to grow up and launch. Siblings, however, may or may not have such a wish. They may feel gratified by having authority over younger siblings or watching another child suffer consequences that they manage to avoid. Or, they can reproach themselves if they weren't able to save a sibling from harm. They may feel survival guilt if they are the one who got away or succeeded, and shame if they are the one who has not managed to get their lives together, they "compare and despair." These are the kinds of feelings that mount in silence and can create sibling competition that lasts and lasts. "One of the most profound effects siblings have on you," says Jeffrey Kluger in *The Sibling Effect*, "is that area of conflict resolution skills, that area of relationship formation and maintenance."

We learn how to negotiate with our siblings: how to share, stick up for ourselves, fight fair (or not), and how to have fun and hang out. But children need adult help to learn how to play fair.

Research by Alfred Adler, a psychoanalyst in the first half of the twentieth century, saw sibling dynamics as the center of family life and personality development. Adler argued that "Social comparisons and power dynamics in families, in particular sibling rivalry for family resources, were fundamental influences on personality development." He felt that in an attempt to manage feelings of competition, siblings "differentiate or de-identify, [by] developing different qualities and choosing different niches." (Susan M. McHale, Kimberly A. Updegraff, and Shawn D. Whiteman) In other words, kids each look for their own territory in which to shine or take over. If "good athlete" is taken, maybe the next child goes for "good student." If "beautiful" is granted to one sister, maybe other sisters try for "smart" or "social" or "fun" or even "screw-up." More recent studies have continued to support Adler's theories.

Kids compete in even the most well-adjusted families and it can serve their development well. But when a family is in chaos, the competition takes on more intensity. "Children indirectly shape their brothers' and sisters' characteristics and behaviors by serving as sources of social comparison, and from a very young age they attend to the ways in which their parents treat them, relative to their siblings." (Ibid) They watch each other to see who gets more of Dad's praise or Mom's attention. Who got that special trip somewhere or a present that was more valuable than the one I got? When parents play favorites or make some children little partners or confidents and grant them special status, family unity suffers, and individuals do, too.

Sibling Envy and Competition

Children very naturally long to be the entire focus of their mother's or father's attention. The child mind is full of fantasy: "My mother/father loves me best. I am her favorite, and therefore I am the best." Every child wishes to be primary with their mother or father and the only beneficiary of their favor. When a child has what D. W. Winnecott refers to as a "good enough" mother, that mother or father will help them to live through the profoundly disappointing awareness that love, at least sibling love, is shared love.

When, however, siblings have the fantasy or even the reality of seeing their brothers and sisters get what they themselves want as their own, when sibling number two is born and the mother's lap gets taken over by a new baby for example, the older sibling can feel neglected and forgotten, and their hurt and envy can turn into hatred and rage. "You took away what was mine! I see the gaze of my mother's love shining on you, not me. The smile and joy that once came my way is now turned in your direction. You have stolen what was mine, you are bad, I hate you." This can set up a belief that there is a finite amount of love which can be extrapolated into thinking that there is a finite amount of joy, money, and happy days. We can go through life feeling as if someone else's gain is our loss, that we're somehow being deprived.

In a family where the parents have enough love and time to go around, children eventually learn that sharing love does not mean being left out in the cold. That sharing love, in fact, can create more love. Or, at least it doesn't have to feel deeply diminishing. But when the child feels that their feelings of yearning are not seen, cared about, or met with equal love, they can feel like they live on the dark side of the moon. They may feel that someone else is getting all of their light, and they are left to grope through the darkness alone. It takes a "good enough" parent to help the child not to feel neglected and forgotten.

Grandchildren of Addicts (GCAs): How ACAs Pass Down Pain

We used to think addiction skipped a generation. I am not sure that's the full story. What happens is that growing up with addiction (and ACEs and relational disconnection) traumatizes us. But we've seen firsthand what alcohol and drugs can do to otherwise fine, upstanding, and loving people—our parents, for example. And we make a vow never to become an addict, and maybe we don't. But we may still need substantial help working through the very real pain we experienced as children.

As ACAs, we might confuse the wounded child that *lives inside of us* with the child we're raising. We may misinterpret our own child's pain. We over-read signals and protect in our child what actually went unprotected in us.

ACAs can make very loyal, loving parents, who are unaware of the unresolved pain that we're passing down through another generation. We can be emotionally blind to the ways in which we make our children the unsuspecting carriers of our own unresolved pain, shame, grudges, and unmet needs.

As ACAs, we may have trouble seeing ourselves as the one causing other people pain. We think, *Wait a minute. I was the victim here, why should I have to do all of this work to heal the problems that my dysfunctional family saddled me with?*

If we're not healthy psychologically but unable to see it, admit it, work with it, or acknowledge our own dysfunction, we may identify in another person what we're blind to, ashamed of, or afraid of in ourselves. We may even see ourselves as compassionate and caring, trying to get someone—who in truth we've been scapegoating or gaslighting—"help." In this way, we successfully externalize our disowned problems and pin them on someone else. Then we set about fixing in that other person what needs fixing within us. We create scapegoats or symptom bearing children or codependents all over again. Pathology or unresolved issues show up in our children and get passed down through another generation.

The Intergenerational Chain of Pain

If, as ACAs, we recreate our unconscious pain in the next generation, in GCAs, then the next generation may reach for drugs, alcohol, food, sex, or whatever to manage that pain. What appears to be some recessive addict gene that "skips" a generation is really unresolved pain making its way through to our children, to the next generation, actually turning on those alcoholic genes through the relational dynamics of our unresolved trauma. It's the epigenetics of addiction.

ACAs may carry along a habit of externalizing pain and making it about someone or something other than ourselves. Accepting that we ourselves have deep issues that need addressing can be hard for us, and this can block us from taking our first steps into recovery. And so rather than recover, we repeat. We pass down the pain that we still do not acknowledge. Our untreated PTSD impacts the way that we parent.

Maybe we model what we got and treat our kids the way we were treated. Or we do the opposite; if we felt abandoned, we smother our kids; if we felt deprived, we overindulge them. If we felt we were raised too strictly, we don't give our kids enough healthy limits, direction, and boundaries, again the 0–10 and 10–0 extreme modes of functioning that characterize trauma. As ACAs, we tell our GCA kids about our difficult childhoods, so we seem to be aware of ourselves. But without some kind of treatment, we all too often just pass down the pain and trauma *that remains unconscious*, without awareness.

For the GCA, this can be very confusing. At least we as ACAs have the addict to point to as the problem, but the grandchildren of the addict, the GCAs, don't. They may in some way become unconscious carriers of their ACA parent's lack of emotional regulation around pain and anger or neediness. ACAs remember can alternate between neediness and fierce independence. And because we're stuck in childhood, we forget that we're the grown-ups, so we don't realize the impact we're having on our kids. We may want our children to *be* the good relationships that we longed for. But it's not fair to them; they need parents not pals.

One likely type of parent who might want to locate their "illness" in another, are those whose self-image is idealized. Perhaps the image they have of themselves is that of a very good person, and they cannot face the sides of themselves that they feel to be weak, scared, shame-filled or "bad." They may even see themselves as superior, or they may glamorize their own particular set of defenses. Coldness and indifference become "boundaries," or lack of empathy becomes "tough love," aggression becomes "forthrightness, a can-do attitude," meanness becomes "straight talk," and so on. They take recovery-sounding words and misapply them.

Denial can be very cunning. Remember, we can be scared to let our guard down, to look underneath our defenses, because when we constructed these defenses in the first place, they felt protective and vital. The epigenetics then are that the GCA may carry the kind of emotional and psychological pain that their parents deny is inside of them. It leaks out in a myriad of ways that the GCAs become the unwitting receptacle for and it's confusing for them, after all, their parents didn't drink, did they?

Journaling Page

FOR PARENTS: (NOTE: if you are not a parent you can do this exercise thinking of any young people in your life who you care about. USE YOUR IMAGINATION AND ...)

1. Identify an age in your children's (or young person's) lives that is difficult for you, that tugs on something inside of you. This often manifests as excessive worry for your child at that age, concern that something is amiss or will go wrong for them. What is the age and what do you imagine might happen in their lives?

_____

_____

_____

_____

2. Now close your eyes and imagine yourself at that same age. What was going on around you? What was occurring in YOUR life at that age? Describe what you see with your inner eye.

_____

_____

_____

_____

3. Feel the feelings that you felt then, think the thoughts that you thought then. Journal a little about your thoughts and feelings.

_____

_____

_____

_____

_____

4. Now ask yourself, "is there something from this time in MY life that is making me extra anxious about this time in MY CHILD'S (or your person's) life? Am I projecting or even creating pain that is more about me than my child? Write a few sentences about that.

_____

_____

_____

_____

_____

5. If the answer is "yes" then see if you can allow more memory to come up, more feelings, more thoughts; let a fuller picture emerge. Describe that fuller picture.

_____

_____

_____

_____

_____

6. Now let yourself just sit with this awareness, you might feel some pain because if you shut something down it was likely because it hurt. You might feel some guilt because you realize that you've been putting your own pain on your kid. You might feel some confusion because stuff is coming up and dis-equilibrating you. You might feel some relief because it feels so good to connect the dots. Write a few sentences about what you're feeling, now.

_____

_____

_____

_____

_____

7. Now be good to yourself, don't rush to your child (or young person) to explain yourself, just sit with this new awareness and breathe through it, visualize comforting yourself at this age. Then take your own hand and let the adult in you, take the child in you, out of harm's way. What would you like to say to the child inside of you?

_____

_____

_____

_____

_____

_____

_____

_____

_____

_____

_____

_____

_____

_____

_____

_____

_____

_____

_____

_____

8. Okay now relax, rest if you can or just continue through your day and let this go, the awareness will continue to come, just let them and remember to be good to yourself and to breathe through the feelings.

Sharon Wegscheider-Cruse's
Addicted Family Roles

In the 1980s, Sharon Wegscheider-Cruse, an early voice for often-neglected children of addicted family systems, adapted the roles from family systems theory to the addicted family system, then added her own and they became an industry standard.

"For years, when I was working with younger (grade school) children," recounted Sharon, "I visited schools and observed the outside behavior of the children. The observation was in preparation for the development of programs to bring hope and help to younger children. There were four patterns that emerged over the years as I watched children in study and at play. These patterns of behavior were fairly consistent in both areas. As I began to interview their parents, I observed two additional behaviors. In the families that appeared to be more fluid and more open in communication, the behaviors were more fluid and different children in a family had different roles depending on circumstances. The roles were more fluid as they moved among the children. As the family became more rigid or fixed in their behavior, the roles became more akin to personality patterns, they became more fixed in the children. So roles in healthy family systems tend to be fluid and in rigid family systems, more fixed. In families with fewer children, they took on multiple family roles or in larger family systems, the roles repeated themselves.

The Addict	The addict is obviously the person who is addicted to alcohol or drugs and the definition can also include sex, work, gambling, internet and other forms of compulsive behavior that interfere with healthy life and relationships. These behaviors need to be stopped for recovery to proceed. When the addict enters recovery they are asked to face life without their medicators and to give up their compulsive behaviors. This can feel like climbing Mount Everest and they will need daily supports in place to even consider it. If however addicts can embrace a new design for living they can become profoundly deep and human. They have crossed the line, and lived on the dark side so they have great understanding and tolerance for the "flesh being weak," which can make them kind, understanding and forgiving. And if they really embrace the spiritual part of recovery, they can become very beautiful individuals, gifts to the world and have a great sense of humanity, it's foibles and it's gifts along with the absurd and unusual sides of life.
The Enabler	The enabler has made the addict's use possible, they have covered for the addict by denying what was really going on, by distorting and rewriting reality to make it more palatable and by putting their own wish for not rocking the boat over everyone and everything else. Enablers are used to having the problem focused elsewhere. In recovery they will need to own their part of the pathology, they need to back up and see their own depression, anxiety, narcissism or needs for perfection and own them as their own rather than make them about someone else. This can be very hard for an enabler and they are at risk for confusing self care and good boundaries for selfishness and aloofness. The enabler has to learn to feel "fairly" to apportion their part of the problem to themselves and stop taking everyone else's inventory. If they do find good recovery, there can be deep relief for them and a great deal of freed up energy and even love.
The Hero	The hero's job is to bring dignity to the family by achieving or having qualities that are highly valued by the parents, perhaps looks, intelligence or talent. They may have a sense of superiority over siblings and they are used to and perhaps dependent upon an unusual amount of parental approval. The hero may have trouble admitting they need help because they need to be perfect and they don't want to lose their hero status. Once they do join however, they can become dedicated to doing a really good job with recovery.

The Scapegoat	The scapegoat, also called the "symptom bearer" or the "identified patient" wears and manifests the dysfunction that the family is trying not to look at. They give the family someone else to focus on which helps the family to keep their anxiety and fears hidden. The scapegoat however, often gets into recovery early because they have already been forced to see themselves as a problem person so they are relieved to think they can get out of this role. The hard thing for them is to let go of their anger and resentment, they get stuck in it because it's part of their role to act out anger and resentment and to gain a sense of power and place in doing so. To recover, they need to develop new and more positive habits or thoughts, feelings and actions. Meditation can be a gamechanger as it teaches the scapegoat to sit with painful emotions without acting them out and also in the sitting through, the may learn to see their feelings more reflectively.
The Lost Child	The lost child is the one who no one needs to notice or "worry about." They tend to stay under the radar, not complain, and solve their own problems. The upside of the role is that the lost child can have a highly developed and nourishing inner world that they can retreat into that holds them, they can often reflect and mentate. But they have come to rely on retreating into their own world in order to feel good and safe so they can have a hard time trusting, as they learned not to rely on their family net-work. In recovery, the lost child will need to process their feelings of being lost. They can learn to trust realistically, with boundaries, that trusting doesn't have to be perfect or 100 percent. And they can learn to reach out and ask for help.
The Mascot	The mascot can be very quick, charming, funny and a good person in a group. They can be very well liked. Their job in the family is to break tension, to entertain the family by acting out their anxieties, to lighten the load. The mascot breaks the tension with humor or charm. However, the mascot can feel powerless in the family system because their charm and humor never really worked to bring anything more than temporary relief and they have learned to gain power and place by, in a sense, taking care of others. They need to learn how to take their own power back and not care as much what others think. For the mascot to get into therapy it helps if therapy is fun, if they are allowed to laugh, to prank. The world of recovery can be filled with humor and spirituality and a fun person in a group is as welcome in group therapy as a party, so the mascot can help groups to bond and have fun together while at the same time learning to take care of their own needs. By taking care of themselves within the context of a group, the mascot can learn to use their unique abilities con-sciously and when they choose to, rather than be sacrificed to the needs of the group.

Family Role Reflections

1. Which role or roles do you identify with? Name each role and describe how you see yourself playing it or them.

_____

_____

_____

_____

2. What are the downsides of playing this role or these roles?

_____

_____

_____

_____

3. Are there hidden or overt benefits of playing them?

_____

_____

_____

_____

4. What do you imagine were the benefits to your family system of you playing that role or those roles?

_____

_____

_____

_____

5. What do you feel were the hidden lessons and gifts of the role you played?

_____

_____

_____

_____

CHAPTER NINE

Treasure Your Triggers: Let Your Pain Light a Path

The wound is where the light enters you.

—Rumi

The unhealed traumatized mind when triggered, has a short fuse. It makes mountains out of molehills. It assumes offense where none was intended. It projects unconscious pain, making it about anything and everything outside of the self, just to get rid of it, to avoid having to sit with it for even a second more than it finds tolerable. It lives in extremes, shooting from 0–10 and 10–0 with no speed bumps in between, black and white, no middle ground. It goes from numbness and shut down to high-voltage intensity and then back again. It is, in other words, dysregulated.

When I see someone dividing people or life or the world into black and white, with no shades of gray, I look for trauma. When I see someone erecting walls of defense, or using "boundaries" as battering rams, deciding a relationship is on or off, good or bad, saying something is "in my life" or "gone forever," I look for trauma. This kind of black-and-white thinking is part and parcel of the traumatized mind that thinks and feels in extremes, that has not found adequate healing to be able to live in an emotional midrange of 4, 5, and 6.

When ACAs get triggered by someone's behavior and it activates their unconscious unhealed pain, they may read that person's behavior in black-and-white terms because their own emotional response is dysregulated inside of them. They can't right-size their reactions. They haven't translated their pain into words and elevated it into consciousness, so it's still numbed out, split out of consciousness. Then the other person stimulates that dysregulated/numb pain and *splat*, it goes onto them. That person suddenly goes from being all good to all bad, right to wrong, nice to mean. They become the enemy. This psychic splitting is often linked to trauma, so when I see it, I investigate further. I ask questions like, "What is this situation bringing up for you? Are these feelings that you've had before? Tell me more about that, paint a picture, who was there, how old were you, what was going on and how did you feel at the time?"

When Intimacy Is Triggering

What triggers us sends up a red flag marking the spot of unprocessed pain. Getting really triggered can hurtle us into that confused, vulnerable, and helpless inner kid space all over again. In much the same way as the sound of a car backfiring can throw a soldier back to a battlefield of years past. Our gunshot sound is intimacy and deep connection, fears of feeling close, of connecting on a deep level. Fear of humiliation, of our own deep neediness and vulnerability. Fear of exposure.

The very feelings of closeness, dependency, and vulnerability that are so much a part of intimacy can trigger us into the same defensive behaviors that we used as kids to say safe, to feel whole rather than splintered.

We can be remarkably blind to our own extreme modes of functioning when our trauma mind gets triggered. But when those unconscious feelings get activated, they can become very big, very fast. And we may have a hard time right-sizing them and regulating them once they are stirred up.

Over-Sensitized to Stress

"Years of research has told us that people do become sensitized to stress and that this sensitization actually alters physical patterns in the brain," says Seymour Levine, PhD, of the University of Delaware. "That means that once sensitized, the body...does not respond to stress the same way in the future. We may produce too many excitatory chemicals or too few calming ones; either way we are responding inappropriately." (Carpi, 2016) In other words, we're over-responding (or under-responding) to feelings inside of ourselves or situations that might otherwise be more easily managed.

However, when we *see the trigger as the cause,* we don't make the enlightening associations *between the past and present* that would free us from repeating and passing down pain. We remain unaware of the hurt or anger from the past, that is fueling our overreaction in the present. This is how we recreate our most painful dynamics from the past in our relationships today. This is how we pass pain down mindlessly through the generations. We shout the words at someone today that we longed to say many years ago. We feel the pain we shut down in childhood, in our relationship interactions today.

But it's at the wrong time, in the wrong place, and with the wrong person. So we burden our relationships of today with unconscious, unresolved pain from yesterday.

Why Trauma Memories
Can Remain Unconscious

If a memory was never processed with the thinking mind, we don't know where that memory fits or even that the memory belongs to the past.

This should make a lightbulb go off in our heads. Why? Well, because if the language part of the brain wasn't functioning at the moment of the traumatic experience, we didn't translate that experience into words. It remains locked inside of us as a sensorial/body memory. We never found ways to describe it and thus elevate it into conscious level where we could think about it, where we could reflect on it. Where we could make meaning and learn from our experience. We didn't then, after understanding it, file it away in its appropriate context with a time and place stamped onto it. Rather, it lives inside of us, a jumble of sense impressions with no unifying meaning, an unconscious body memory. That's why songs, smells, sounds, or sights can be so triggering. They are sensorial markers, they hold unprocessed experience, and woven in with the sense impressions is the way we felt at the time of the trauma.

"Neurons that fire together wire together" When it comes to trauma memories, fear is often a predominant feeling associated with the sense impressions, along with the feeling that we need to self-protect. That's why when we're in the midst of a painful interaction say with our spouse or child, we can get scared and triggered into that old, pain space from yesteryear. The more all of these elements of memory fire together, the more a pattern of reaction is formed and strengthened, the more they "wire together." So repeated small fights and disconnections for example, make us more likely to keep fighting and disconnecting. *But those spaces and places inside of us that get triggered hold a lot of information about what hurt us and how much something once hurt.* However sometimes the only way we know this, is because of our extreme reactions from 0-10, that is we shut down, withdraw and feel nothing, or we feel way too much. So even if we're blind to our pain, we can use our triggered, fear stained over reactions as an indicator that something's up. When we get triggered in other words, we need to stop, look and listen.

This is why triggers are treasures. They reveal to us what we hold in our own inner darkness, in our psychic blind spots. Partnering and parenting are nature's way of giving us a second chance to repair our own childhood wounds. The feelings of deep attachment warm up those spots inside of us where we felt warm and connected or rejected and disconnected. So when we get triggered we can take the conscious road or the unconscious road. We can use what is being triggered as a light that is being shed in the darkness of our own unconscious. Or, we can explode or implode or act out rather than talk out. We have a choice.

How the Body and Mind Play Off of Each Other

We can get caught in endless negative feedback loops within our own minds, we go on negative jags in which emotions and thoughts that we have experienced simultaneously in the past, become felt together in the present, they become associated. For example, closeness might get paired with fear, rejection with shame, criticism/meddling/superiority with anger, or excitement with potential disappointment. And then we get caught in a negative narrative, "nothing ever goes right for me," "other people are selfish, badly intended." As we feel and re-feel these pairings, they become reinforced. "Neurons that fire together wire together" is the well-used adage coined by Canadian neuropsychologist Donald Hebb, known for his work in associative learning. (Carpi, 2016) This wiring and firing together of associative brain pathways can pair thoughts and feelings (or impulses).

Negative and traumatic thoughts tend to "loop"—they play themselves over and over until you do something consciously to stop them. The more these negative thoughts loop, the stronger the neural pathways become, and the more difficult it becomes to stop them! This is why thoughts that cause depression, anxiety, panic, obsessions, and compulsions can become so difficult to combat. And along the way, these thoughts stir up emotional as well as physiological reactions. (Carpi, 2016)

This strengthening of negative thoughts through repetition can send us into what can become a downward shame, rage, or pain spiral in which negative thoughts and images can stimulate physiological body sensations (read: queasy stomach, shortness of breath, pounding heart/head, tight chest, throbbing, etc.). Then these disturbing physiological body sensations stir up more disturbing thoughts, feelings, and mental imagery or memories. In this way, we can sail down into a black hole in which physiological sensations stimulate anxiety-provoking mental and sensorial reactions and those reactions stimulate more body sensations. They play off of each other.

Self-Fulfilling Prophecies: Priming, Automatic Recollection, and More

The phenomenon of priming refers to memories that are stored and then re-stimulated. Schemas refer to sequences of information stored in long-term memory. These schemas tend to be primed together. Say you felt rejected as a child, so much so that the feelings stored with and around rejection became associated in your memory bank. You might be primed for rejection. The same behavior, in other words, that would feel rejecting to you might not be read as rejecting to someone else who isn't "primed" for the pain of a rebuff. So priming is a part of what we refer to as implicit (read unconscious or automatic) memory. Your implicit memory uses past experience to "remember" things without having to think about them. So the recall is almost automatic and often unconscious. And with implicit memory, it doesn't matter how long ago these experiences occurred.

Dr. Joe Dispenza puts it this way in *Breaking the Habit of Being Yourself* (2013):

> Every time you respond to your familiar reality by re-creating the
> same mind (that is, turning on the same nerve cells to make the brain

work in the same way), you "hardwire" your brain to match the custom-ary conditions in your personal reality, be they good or bad. Hebb's credo demonstrates that if you repeatedly activate the same nerve cells, then each time they turn on, it will be easier for them to fire in unison again. Eventually those neurons will develop a long-term relationship. So when I use the word *hardwired,* it means that clusters of neurons have fired so many times in the same ways that they have organized themselves into specific patterns with long-lasting connections. The more these networks of neurons fire, the more they wire into static routes of activity. In time, whatever the oft-repeated thought, behavior, or feeling is, it will become an automatic, unconscious habit. When your environment is influencing your mind to that extent, *your habitat becomes your habit.* So if you keep thinking the same thoughts, doing the same things, and feeling the same emotions, you will begin to hardwire your brain into a finite pattern that is the direct reflection of your finite reality. Consequently, it will become easier and more natural for you to reproduce the same mind on a moment-to-moment basis. This innocent response cycle causes your brain and then your mind to reinforce even further the particular reality that is your external world. The more you fire the same circuits by reacting to your external life, the more you'll wire your brain to be equal to your personal world. You'll become neurochemically attached to the conditions in your life. In time, you'll begin to think "in the box," because your brain will fire a finite set of circuits that then creates a very specific mental signature. This signature is called your *personality.* (Dispenza, 2013)

Mercifully, Hebb's research also laid foundations for what is referred to as neuroplasticity, or the brain's ability to grow and change well into old age, which is why recovery works so well. If we can take responsibil-ity for our own overreaction rather than hold the other guy responsible, something magical happens. We unlock ourselves from the cycle of externalizing our pain, and we can make choices about new strategies for dealing with it. We can grow and strengthen new, positive neuronal pathways. We learn new ways of dealing with situations that used to confound us.

To Feel or Not to Feel

Jeffrey Smith, MD, in his article "Emotions: To Avoid or to Feel," talks about two ways of experiencing feelings once they are triggered, as taking one of two forks in the road. When the feeling comes up:

> One choice is to do something to make the pain go away. The other is to face it. What is critical is that this choice has consequences. If you choose to avoid the feeling, then no healing or growth takes place. The feeling is simply put aside till next time and sick patterns remain unchanged. Meanwhile, the things that have been done to make the feeling go away have their consequences, which play out in the real adult world. Think of acting out in some way like cutting, obsessing, or picking a fight with someone, etc. It is easy to be distracted by the consequences and dealing with them, and soon the original feeling is far away. On the other hand, if you take the other fork and face the feeling, holding it for a few seconds, then permanent healing can take place. This is what I have referred to as "catharsis," in honor of Freud's original description in 1893. By doing this over and over, the pain will lose its power and no longer dominate life. (Smith, 2017)

Avoidance is a common outgrowth of trauma. We avoid the feelings or situations that create pain and insecurity within us. People spend a lifetime avoiding all sorts of painful feelings and living them out, as Carl Jung puts it, "as fate." If only we could understand that the pain we're creating is worse than the pain we're avoiding. It can take a few minutes to feel hidden pain. It can take a few decades to undo the consequences of avoiding it. It's "Recovery 101."

Riding Out the Limbic Storm: From Reliving to Repairing

When you are in a triggered state, it is not the time to work something out *with someone else*. It is the time to work something out *with yourself!*

A triggered moment can be a wonderful time to gain deep insight into ourselves, but it may be just the wrong time to try to work something out with someone else.

When we're somehow *reminded* of something we found traumatic or we're in a relationship dynamic that feels threatening, our body can act as if the trauma is happening all over again. We "relive" it, we enter into fight/flight/freeze mode. Having some quick tricks to fall back on, some training, can help us to tolerate these moments without digging ourselves deeper into them and behaving in ways we later regret, without "living them out as fate." Antonio Damasio, neuroscientist and author of *Looking for Spinoza: Joy, Sorrow, and the Feeling Brain*, describes that when we get triggered, at that moment our breathing and heart rate quicken, or we can stop breathing and hold our breath. Our muscles can be flooded with blood and our body with adrenaline to enable a quick flight or fight, and we feel a constriction in our gut. The sooner we can recognize that this is a cascading pattern that we're sliding into, the more successful we can be in turning it around.

Choose whatever works for you, some things to do when you're feeling triggered that can help you to down-regulate and will give you the time and space to make valuable connections can be:

- *Breathe.* Go to your breath: breathe in and out slowly and mindfully.
- *Re-Regulate.* Say to yourself, "I'm having an out-sized, emotional reaction. I'm triggered. I'm dis-regulated."
- *Relax.* Breathe and consciously let go of the tension in your body; breathe it out.

- *Detach.* Allow your mind to move father away, and witness your thoughts as they move past your inner eye without trying to control or respond to them.
- *Center.* Drop your awareness to the center of your body just below your gut area, and breathe into that area.
- *Focus.* Choose a mantra or a word for how you'd rather feel and repeat it; breathe and allow yourself to experience a shift.
- *Stamp Your Feet.* Feel the weight of your feet or stamp them softly and connect with the ground, saying, "left, right, left, right."
- *How Important Is It?* Ask yourself, "How important will this be in five years?"
- *Warm Water.* If you're with others, excuse yourself and wash your hands slowly in warm water, or do the dishes, or take a warm bath if you are free to do so.
- *Make a Graceful Exit.* Say to someone else, "I'd like to continue this, but I need a quick break to attend to _____ *(fill in the blank; it can be anything that will give you a few moments to compose yourself)*.
- *Change Your Attitude.* Decide that you are in charge of your own reaction and that you have a choice about what to do with it. You don't have to stay stuck in a knee jerk reaction.

We can learn to use our pain as a path; we can examine what triggers us and follow it to its source. We can observe our reenactment dynamics and mine them for information about the kinds of relational dynamics from our past, that made us go unconscious because they hurt so much. We can allow the transferences that we have laid over someone else to slip form their face just long enough so that we can see the face that they really belong to. And we can pull back our projections to finally feel and understand the feelings we are trying so hard to get rid of.

Our wounded child may have frozen spots along our developmental continuum. When we operate from these frozen places, our reactions may be very immature. Processing this pain and then making conscious and disciplined efforts toward more mature and functional thinking is one of the ways that we can become more mature, that we can grow ourselves up! We can listen to that child in us, translate their hurt into grownup thoughts and words, and communicate from there rather than blurting out all of our old pain and rage and then being disappointed and hurt that no one wants to listen. Why would they when we don't even want to listen to ourselves?

My Triggers

Prompt: Fill in the blanks.

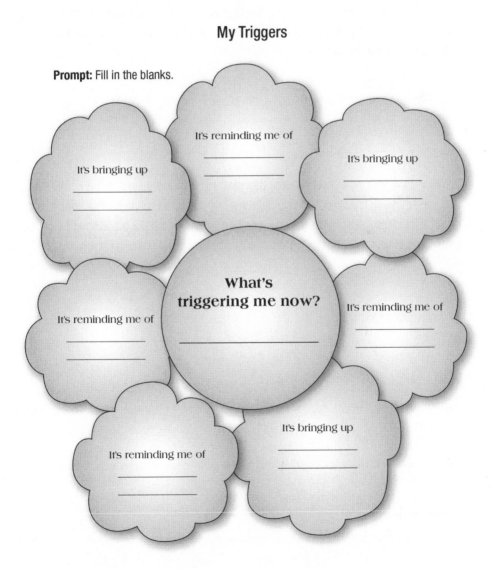

Trigger Inquiry

1. Describe a situation that frequently triggers you, such as feeling criticized, humiliated, hearing others yelling, anger, anxiety, tears, etc. Describe the situation, who's in it, and how you are feeling.

_____

_____

_____

_____

2. Now allow your mind to make any associations with this scene. Is there a time in your past that you feel this may have gotten set up, or a place of origin from which this grew? If so, describe it, where are you, and how you are sitting or standing or being in the situation.

_____

_____

_____

_____

3. Who else is in the situation with you?

_____

_____

_____

4. What do you observe about yourself? Describe, please.

_____

_____

_____

_____

5. What do you observe yourself feeling?

_____

_____

_____

_____

6. What are you thinking?

_____

_____

_____

_____

7. What would you like to do?

_____

_____

_____

_____

8. What would you like to say?

_____

_____

_____

_____

9. Now come back to the present trigger. What are you feeling?

_____

_____

_____

_____

10. How do you act when triggered, what do you do?

_____

_____

_____

_____

11. What do you say when triggered?

_____

_____

_____

_____

12. Do you see similarities between the past and the present?

_____

_____

_____

_____

13. What can you shift or change in your reactions to become more engaged and nourishing both toward yourself and toward someone else?

_____

_____

_____

_____

_____

_____

_____

CHAPTER TEN

Anger: Containing the Explosion

"You will not be punished for your anger,
you will be punished by your anger."

—Buddha

Anger is one of those emotions that can create problems if not understood. We don't know what to do with it, how to manage it, whether it's better to feel it or talk ourselves out of it. Anger can be functional or dysfunctional. Functional anger generally moves a situation forward in some way; we recognize we're angry about something and that motivates us to reassess. Maybe we make a change in the way we're handling a situation, or shift our expectations so we're not setting ourselves up for disappointment, and subsequently, anger. Or we process our angry feelings with someone we trust and make some choices about what to do with them.

Dysfunctional anger, on the other hand, can be a place we get swept into, where our anger seems to multiply and feed on itself until it has a life of its own. Though there is not a diagnostic category that addresses anger disorders specifically, problems with anger and its dark companion rage, can create many issues both in intimate relationships and the workplace. Because it is a somewhat denied emotion in our society, we have not developed ways of working with it that allow it to be functional rather than dysfunctional. It simmers, boils up, explodes, hides or lays in wait.

Anger is also often used as a defense against feeling our own deeper feelings of fear and sadness. We've developed a habit of not feeling our hurt or we feel too vulnerable saying we're hurt so we use anger as a defense. Expressing anger in a safe, therapeutic context can open the door to grief, it can unblock feelings that keep someone stuck, and the sadness and yearning underneath the anger can begin to come out. This can help to relieve anxiety and depression as things start to move.

A more dysfunctional expression of anger might be when we continue, in a sense, to retraumatize ourselves with our own cycle of anger or negativity. We get angry, in a state of high stress, or we get locked into a negative narrative and our anger or negativity makes the current situation we're in very complicated to work through. When this occurs, other emotions associated with the grief process, like sadness, hurt and a feeling of "falling apart" never emerge. We use anger to protect our feelings of vulnerability and it keeps us from exposing and processing the kinds of emotions that would help us to heal and grow.

The Angry Body

We experience anger in our bodies as well as in our minds, which is why it feels like it takes us over. When we get triggered into anger, our heart rate accelerates, our blood pressure rises, and our rate of breathing increases. Our body's muscles tense up. We suddenly feel all of these disquieting sensations surging through us, our face may flush as increased blood flows through our limbs to ready us to take evasive action or to fight. Along with increased blood flow, stress/energy hormones like adrenaline and noradrenaline are released in our brain/bodies that give us the burst of energy that's behind our knee-jerk desire to take immediate, self-protective action. Another very interesting thing happens that explains a lot about why angry people act the way they act, *our attention narrows and becomes locked onto the target of our anger; soon we can pay attention to nothing else.*

The same lingering arousal that keeps us primed for more, anger can also interfere with our ability to clearly remember details of our angry outburst. A certain level of arousal is vital for efficient remembering. As any student knows, it is difficult to learn new material while sleepy. Moderate arousal levels help the brain to learn and enhance memory, concentration, and performance. There is an optimum level of arousal that benefits memory, however, and when arousal exceeds that optimum level, it makes it more difficult for new memories to be formed. High levels of arousal (such as are present when we are angry) can also significantly decrease our ability to concentrate. This is why it is difficult to remember details of really explosive arguments.

The Rage State: Hijacking Our Brains

Rage can hijack our brains, it can take us over, obliterating reason and blowing past ordinary boundaries. And we can be almost in a blackout which is why people who rage often don't remember what they were like while raging and they minimize their effect on others. "During rage attacks...those parts of the brain that are central to feeling and expressing anger, such as the amygdala and the hypothalamus, commandeer the rest of the brain. In this wholesale takeover, the cerebral cortex is overwhelmed, and restraint and reasoning are impossible.... Although rage—by which I mean anger that is extreme, immoderate or unrestrained —may be adaptive as a response to severe threat, in most situations it destroys much more than it accomplishes," says Dr. Norman Rosenthal in *The Emotional Revolution*. Chronic rage might also be an indicator of depression. It's been estimated that 40 percent of those suffering from rage attacks also suffer from clinical depression.

Sudden angry outbursts can also be a part of PTSD or unresolved grief. Rosenthal continues, "Dr. Martin Teicher and colleagues at Harvard have found that adults who were abused as children, whether verbally, physically, or sexually, show brain wave changes over the temporal lobe of the cerebral cortex. These changes resemble those seen in people with documented seizures in the temporal lobe, which surrounds the limbic structures.... Teicher suggests that early traumatic experiences might kindle seizure-type activity in this area, resulting in a storm of electrical activity in the emotional part of the cerebral cortex... the end result could be a brain that is cocked and all too ready to fire off a limbic storm."

The Effect of High Hostility (HO) Scored on Health and Relationships

Much in the way that salt makes a person with high blood pressure get a dangerous increase, while salt for a person with normal blood pressure causes no increase, a high HO person gets more stressed out when they are angry (or more angry when they are stressed out) than a low HO person. People who have high hostility (HO) scores just seem to have a harder time in life than those with lower scores. For one thing, they suffer more internally when they get angry and the cumulative effects of their anger last longer, they become "primed" for angry reactions.

In Finland, persons with high HO scores had a four times higher death rate and similar patterns when it came to cancer. Timothy Smith, a University of Utah researcher, found that students with high HO scores reported more hassles and negative life events, and had less social support than those with lower scores. In the same study, married couples with high HO scores had more "dominating acrimonious interchanges than those with low HO scores."

David Masci, founder of Associated Couples for Marriage Enrichment (ACME), cites anger as one of the key issues in faltering marriages: a failure to manage anger issues reasonably well, which results in too many or too few disagreements. Couples who cannot deal well with anger tend to withdraw from intimacy and lose passion. In a study of hostile workers at a financial management firm, seventy-five men and women with average ages of forty, reported experiencing:

- Greater stress in interpersonal aspects of work
- Less job satisfaction
- Negative views of work relationships

Anger also creates problems in the work environment. A Lawrence, Kansas study of middle-aged women with high levels of hostility (HO) experienced:

- More stressful job experiences
- More daily stresses and tensions
- More role conflicts, conflicts with co-workers
- Feelings that skills were being underutilized

Simmering Down

If anger has a physiological preparation phase during which our resources are mobilized for a fight, it also has a wind-down phase as well. We start to relax back toward our resting state when the target of our anger is no longer accessible or an immediate threat. It is difficult to relax from an angry state, however. The adrenaline-caused arousal that occurs during anger lasts a very long time (many hours, sometimes days), and lowers our anger threshold, making it easier for us to get angry again. Though we do calm down, it takes a very long time for us to return to our resting state. During this slow cool-down period we are more likely to get very angry in response to minor irritations that normally would not bother us.

"Getting control over our anger means learning ways to help our prefrontal cortex get the upper hand over our amygdala so that we have control over how we react to angry feelings inside of us and/or coming towards us from someone else. If the amygdala handles emotion, the prefrontal cortex handles judgment. The amygdala "is involved in the processing of emotions such as fear, anger, and pleasure. The amygdala is also responsible for determining what memories are stored and where the memories are stored in the brain. It is thought that this determination is based on how huge an emotional response an event evokes. For example, when we hear an unpleasant sound, the amygdala heightens our perception of the sound. This heightened perception is deemed distressing and memories are formed associating the sound with unpleasantness.

If the noise startles us, we have an automatic flight or fight response. This response involves the activation of the peripheral nervous system... [which]...results in accelerated heart rate, dilated pupils, increase in metabolic rate, and increase in blood flow to the muscles. This activity is coordinated by the amygdala and allows us to respond appropriately to danger." (Ibid) It can also mean that when we're activated in this way, we read danger even if it isn't there because our feelings of fear are associated with interactions that felt "dangerous" from the past.

The left prefrontal cortex serves an executive role to keep things under control. Among the many ways to gain some control are relaxation techniques such as breathing (which reduce our arousal and decrease our amygdala activity), mindfulness, and the use of cognitive control techniques which help us practice using our judgment to override our emotional reactions. "How important will this be in five years?" "easy does it", "if it's hysterical, it's historical" are some of the program slogans for moments such as these!

Anger can hide under a lot of rocks, it can leak out under various disguises or burst forward, understanding the many ways in which anger can manifest is another way of helping us to understand and manage it more thoughtfully.

Exploring How Anger Manifests for Me

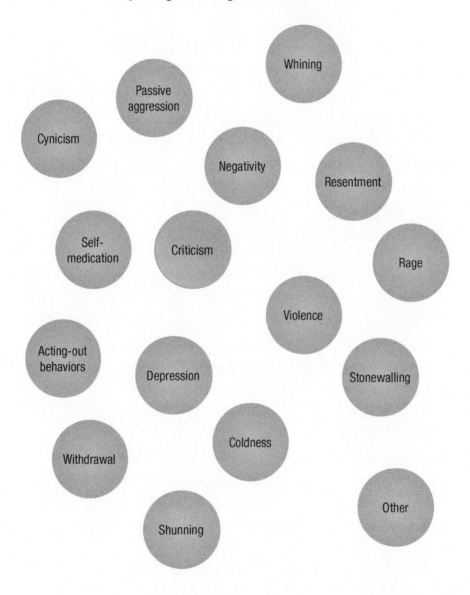

In the following process, you can explore how anger might manifest for you.

Anger Check-In

Which manifestation of anger draws you right now? Please say something about that.

_____

_____

_____

_____

Which form of anger is your "go to"? Share something about why you feel this is the case.

_____

_____

_____

_____

Which form of anger do you fear the most and why?

_____

_____

_____

_____

Which form of anger do you sort of like and why?

_____

_____

_____

_____

Which form of anger do you have trouble dealing with in someone else?

_____

_____

_____

_____

_____

_____

What do you think you could do to manage your anger better?

_____

_____

_____

_____

_____

_____

Understanding Our Psychic Defenses:
Repair, Repair, Repair

The difference between dysfunctional and functional relationships lies, in part, in our ability or lack of ability to repair small and large ruptures and to use emotions that are being triggered as grist for the mill of communication, understanding and healing, rather than as fuel for fights.

So why don't people repair? For starters, in alcoholic families, there is so much unacknowledged hurt, so much denied pain, so much twisted logic, and so much mistrust and rupture caused by horrible behavior, that no one knows where to begin to repair it. And then there is the elephant in the room, the subject that no one will talk about, because talking about it may carry an implicit demand that something be done about it. And we get used to these dysfunctional behavior patterns, they start to feel normal and challenging them feels challenging to our sense of who we are. Family members have been hurt in so many ways and in such strange and far-ranging variety that they have dug their defenses in deep, and they can be quite rigid or self-righteous. They are, in other words, hard pressed to let them go. They have learned to be self-protective, to do whatever they need to do to stay out of harm's way. Staying safe has been and still is paramount and happens in a split second and as the defenses were originally adopted and adapted to cover up so much hurt, anger, and confusion, letting them go feels frightening. And because they were fashioned by a child mind, they can be very immature. If the stressor was chronic, as is so often the case with family problems such as addiction, abuse or neglect, these kinds of defenses likely got mobilized much of the time and are well practiced! We used them because they were reliable, they worked, and they became a mode of functioning, our default positions. So without examining them, they become automatic. Thus when we get triggered, we revert to default, defensive positions that got set up in the past and they get in our way in the present.

Tracing back these defensive patterns is part of the work of recovery. Understanding our own defensive positions so that we can make them transparent and eventually allow them to at least partially dissolve or to gain enough self-awareness so that we don't stay stuck in them is, too.

As we feel in order to heal, we need to ask ourselves what defensive strategies, we used to stay safe and then *shift these behaviors to be more engaged and nourishing both within our relationships and ourselves.* After all, if we constantly brace for danger and rejection, then we are likely to create it. It can become a self-fulfilling prophecy. Shifting negative thinking, feeling, and behavior to more engaged and positive versions of each of them is part of where the gold lies. We can mine pain all we like but if we don't make this crucial shift, change doesn't really happen and hold.

Psychic defenses have been around for a long time and are part of psychoanalytic theory. I am not sure how useful I think labeling is, but these defenses have stood the test of time, and you will probably want to be familiar with them if you are not already.

Splitting (I have referred to this as black-and-white think-ing or all-or-nothing thinking) happens when we can't bring together extremes of positive and negative thinking, feeling, or the qualities in someone or in ourselves and pull them together into a coherent and reality based whole; someone is either all good or all bad. We can also experience splitting as a defense mechanism if we've experienced childhood trauma. We push what pains us out of conscious awareness, we "split it off."

Denial is the refusal to accept a situation or behavior that is happening; it is rewriting it to make it feel more palatable or outright saying that it doesn't exist. It is considered one of the most primitive of the defense mechanisms because it is something that can be part of how children handle painful circumstances. The "looking-good" family that is common when addiction is present can reflect a family in denial.

Dissociation is a psychic defense in which we essentially flee on the inside, we're "gone," and we "leave" in the situation we're in. A person who dissociates can lose track of time or their thought processes or even memories. Dissociation is common when there is childhood abuse. Children cannot leave a situation when an adult is abusing them, they cannot flee physically, so they flee psychically. They may disconnect from the real world for a time and live in another psychic space less cluttered with thoughts, feelings, or memories that feel unbearable.

Somatization happens when we evidence physical symptoms of a psychiatric condition like depression, fear, sadness, or anxiety. It is our body in essence doing our feeling for us, storing pain that we cannot for some reason process more consciously. Emotional pain can manifest as a sore back, stiff neck or muscles, queasiness, body aches, or physical illness.

Repression is a process by which we block something that is occurring, or we block our thoughts and feelings about it. We do this without awareness, and later we may have no access to those thoughts, circumstances, feelings, or impulses that we have repressed. *Repressed memories* are those that have become blurred, altered, and unavailable to us for inner viewing.

Displacement refers to when we "displace" our feelings

toward one person onto another. The child in a painful family cannot express her anger toward her mother to her mother for fear of reprisal or punishment, so she displaces it onto her younger brother or sister. Likewise, the parent who cannot get angry at his or her boss comes home and kicks the dog or yells at their child.

Intellectualization is when we use excessive thinking or get very heady. Rather than deal with our painful emotions, we intellectualize them to distance ourselves from the impulse, event, or behavior. If, for example, we receive a painful diagnosis, we focus endlessly on details of treatment rather than feel our concern, fear, or pain around the illness. Or with family addiction, we talk about emotions, situations or diagnoses, as if there were no feeling attached to them.

Rationalization is the use of feeble but seemingly plausible arguments either to justify or make something that feels too challenging and difficult more acceptable to us. For example, a sibling is jealous of their more-successful sibling but rationalizes that successful people aren't very happy or that they themselves have superior values, and their sibling is a less "good" person than they are.

Regression is when we fall back in psychological time to a younger state. We tend to do it if we're stressed. When our thoughts, feelings, and impulses are too triggering for us to handle, when we're on psychic or emotional overload, we can regress. An example of this might be an adolescent who is fearful, anxious, or angry and at the same time dealing with growing sexual impulses might revert to bedwetting. Or, an adult when overwhelmed with pressure and emotional and psychic stress, might not get out of bed. I see this when ACAs feel angry, humiliated, or hurt: they lash out like children with blame, rage, and insults, or they can become stubborn, passive-aggressive, or withdrawn. Some people experience parts of therapy/recovery as a regression because they are thrown back into some childhood states as a part of their movement forward. Bursts of growth are often followed by temporary regression, even as we recover. Children may have a regression just after a burst in learning, maturation, or growth, and this is natural.

Compartmentalization is a diluted form of dissociation, wherein parts of oneself are separated from awareness, and we may behave as if the self in each compartment has very different morals or standards from our presenting self. An example might be an otherwise loving partner cheats on his wife and compartmentalizes his two value systems, keeping them distinct and unintegrated while also remaining unconscious of the cognitive dissonance within him as a result of very divergent/unintegrated behaviors.

Reaction formation is the converting of unwanted or dangerous thoughts, feelings, or impulses into their opposites. For instance, someone who is very angry with their boss and would like to quit their job may instead be overly kind and generous toward their boss and express a desire to keep working there forever. They are not capable of expressing the negative emotions of dissatisfaction or anger and unhappiness, and instead becomes overly kind to publicly demonstrate their lack of anger and unhappiness. It might also be seen as a form of "undoing."

Idealization, as the name sounds, occurs when a person attributes exaggeratedly positive qualities to themselves or others. If a child is frightened by a parent, they may idealize them as a way to keep their "scary" sides under control, as a way to make them more palatable. In this case the idealization covers up fear.

Throughout the development of a young child, idealization and devaluation are quite normal. As children mature, they become capable of perceiving others as complex, containing both good and bad features. If the developmental stage is interrupted (by early childhood trauma, for example), these defense mechanisms may persist into adulthood. In psychoanalytic theory, idealization in childhood is seen as healthy and normal. However, if parents fail to provide appropriate opportunities for idealization, if they are too distressing or disappointing for the child, the child does not develop beyond a *grandiose* stage. If this is the case, the child may become like the pathological narcissist, dependent on others to provide a sense of self-esteem; to see them in an idealized light. Grandiosity in both the addict and the alcoholic family systems can be a cover up for shame and low self-worth.

Undoing is saying or doing something to "undo" a previous act or thought that we feel uncomfortable with having done, said, or thought. If someone is borderline insulting, they might quickly try to "undo" the effect of the insult with a compliment. It can be seen as a form of apology, though it is not necessarily the "I'm sorry I hurt you," full taking of responsibility that we night hope for if we're on the receiving end. In a family where bad behavior is not properly monitored, someone may go too far being difficult or mean and then be overly sweet to make up for it. Or, an addict who feels guilty for their behavior may use gift giving or effusive generosity, fun, or kindness to "undo" his or her previous hurtful or neglectful behavior. The father who neglects his children may become an "ideal dad" once in a while, hoping to make up for the deficit of caring at other times.

Acting-Out Behaviors can be acting out pain that we have been victim of by becoming the aggressor. The one who lived with rage (silent or overt) becomes the rager, the one who was abused becomes the abuser, or the one who was neglected becomes either overbearingly absorbed in others or neglectful— or alternates between the two. They could also be acting out pain that they cannot talk about in self-destructive, self-sabotaging ways or in ways that are dangerous or cause harm to others.

Projection: We project feelings that we cannot bear to live with onto others and make the feelings we don't want to feel about them or about the relationship, rather than examine where it might be coming from within ourselves. We project emotions from our inner world that we do not want to experience onto something or someone else.

Transferences: We transfer or project the relationship dynamics from a relationship in the past onto a relationship in the present. Transferring unconscious pain from relationships in the past onto new relationships in the present and seeing it as all about the person in the present without making any connections to relationships from the past is part of transference.

Reenactment Dynamics/Passing down the pain: We recreate the painful, unresolved relationship dynamics from childhood that are still frozen and unconscious within us in our relationships with our partners and children, co-workers, and friends, recycling old pain into new relationships.

Self-Medication, in any form, can be conceptualized as a defense against feeling unwanted emotions or conditions. It is an attempt to blot out, turn off, manage, or get away from pain, anxiety, physiological symptoms, thoughts, or depression that we don't wish to experience. This is, of course, true whether someone is engaged in an addiction to drugs and alcohol or a process addiction. As an ACA and as a psychologist I understand that when someone is drunk, if I try to reason with them, I will not get very far. I will be talking to the bottle; they are not available. When someone is locked in any defensive position and unwilling or unable to back up from it, a similar phenomenon is at work. We're talking to unconsciousness.

The distinction between adaptation and maladaptation can be difficult to make, since all coping mechanisms are inward struggles to adapt to life and to master its challenges.

Moving away from defensive positions can be a layered process. We may make some adaptations that are more functional but still have elements of unconsciousness. An indication of this is if we can't back up from our defensive position in any way or examine it. As we say in twelve step rooms, it's "progress not perfection."

But it's all grist for the mill. We can make continued progress and get many things to turn out for the best if we view the circumstances in our lives that are painful as grist for the mill of our own personal and spiritual growth. If we process the feelings that get triggered so that we deepen our understanding of what drives our own over reactions rather than project pain as blame or get lost in acting our behaviors or self-medication.

Understanding My Defenses

Look over the list of defenses and journal a bit about your reactions and responses. Don't overthink it; first impression here may just be most informative!

1. Which defense do you feel you use a lot? Describe how that feels from the inside. When/why do you use it?

_____

_____

_____

_____

2. Which defense draws you for some reason you don't quite understand? Do you have any ideas about why you're pulled to it?

_____

_____

_____

_____

3. Which defense do you feel your family used a lot?

_____

_____

_____

_____

4. Which defense did each of your parents use, and how did you experience that?

_____

_____

_____

_____

_____

_____

5. Do you choose people to be in intimate relationships with whom you use one or more of these defenses? If so, who? Say something about that.

_____

_____

_____

_____

6. Which defense keeps you from feeling as open and comfortable as you'd like in close relationships?

_____

_____

_____

_____

7. Which defense really bothers you when you encounter it in someone else and why?

_____

_____

_____

_____

8. What can you feel, think and do to create a more engaged and nourishing response rather than getting locked in a defensive position?

_____

_____

_____

_____

CHAPTER ELEVEN

Numbing the Pain:
The Connection Between
Trauma and Addiction

Nothing is more desirable than to be
released from an affliction; but nothing is more
frightening than to be divested of a crutch.

—James Baldwin

U sing drugs and alcohol to numb out the emotional, psychological
and physiological pain that gets triggered in us because we don't
feel that we can manage it on our own, is at the core of the connection
between trauma and addiction.

Dr. Anda of the ACE studies refers to a "dose and effect" syndrome,
or how childhood adversity directly correlates to problems later in life;
the more numerous the toxic stress clusters, the more serious and long
term the effects. For example, children who grow up with the trauma
associated with adverse childhood experiences are more likely to drink
and do drugs or have physical or mental health problems as adults.
They may self-medicate their adult child pain, "dosing" themselves with
enough drugs and alcohol, food, sex, and so forth to numb their emotional pain and manage their anxiety or depression.

"One of the pervading symptoms of post-traumatic stress disorder (PTSD) both in soldiers and those who have experienced some form of physical, sexual or emotional abuse, neglect or living with addiction, is the desire to self-medicate with drugs or alcohol," says Bessel van der Kolk, expert on PTSD. This means that if someone has experienced trauma in childhood and has used substances as a mood regulator because their own skills of self-regulation felt compromised, they may be recovering from both *PTSD and addiction* when they give up their substance or behavior.

Similarly, ACAs who were traumatized by living with parental addiction and who themselves became addicts or developed a process/behavioral addiction in order to manage that unconscious pain and resentment will likely be dealing with both in recovery. In other words, they will be getting sober from their addictions and then working on their PTSD. This is why having a very solid support network is so crucial. Appointments with therapists and group psychotherapy happen at specific times and time between them can feel long and lonely. But twelve-step meetings are available very frequently, several times a day in many cities. If not as often in other areas, there is usually a network of people to call when you "need a meeting." When addicts go cold turkey and give up their medicators without doing any of the emotional work to heal their heart wounds, they may become physically sober but not emotionally sober. They may exhibit "dry drunk" behaviors because they are "white knuckling it" they have nothing to dull their pain and they aren't seeking help and support to process, understand and move through it.

Locked in the Cycle of Trauma and Addiction

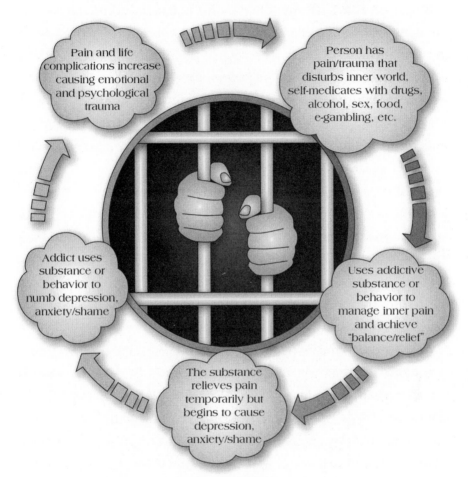

Pain and life complications increase causing emotional and psychological trauma

Person has pain/trauma that disturbs inner world, self-medicates with drugs, alcohol, sex, food, e-gambling, etc.

Addict uses substance or behavior to numb depression, anxiety/shame

Uses addictive substance or behavior to manage inner pain and achieve "balance/relief"

The substance relieves pain temporarily but begins to cause depression, anxiety/shame

Process or Behavioral Addictions

There are more forms of addiction than addiction to drugs and alcohol. We can be locked in an addictive cycle with food, sex, work, or the internet, to name a few. We can also combine medicators to achieve a high, if we only drink in the evening for example, we may use sugar or simple carbs during the day to manage our moods or we might self-medicate with internet porn alongside some marijuana use. It's not always just one thing. Our bodies release natural mood medicators, like dopamine and serotonin. We can activate these soothing and regulating body chemicals through exercise, journaling, thinking positive thoughts, or prayer, to name just a few. But we can also activate them in self-destructive ways that can become addictive, and we call these behavioral or process addictions. These behaviors provide similar short-term rewards as do drugs and alcohol.

"Cross addictions do not always involve drug or alcohol use. Many individuals replace a substance use disorder with an impulse control disorder, which affects the reward pathway of the brain in the same way that substances of abuse do.....Impulsive behaviors such as sex, watching pornography, gambling and eating also cause the brain to release dopamine, producing euphoria and reinforcing the behavior.... The impulsive behavior often becomes the new drug for individuals who develop cross addictions because these behaviors activate the same brain pathway and produce effects similar to those produced by drugs or alcohol." (Dyer, 2019)

According to the National Institute on Drug Abuse (NIDA), process addictions occur when someone becomes addicted to a rewarding behavior that does not involve an addictive substance, such as gambling, sex, or eating. Sometimes referred to as behavioral addictions, or compulsive behaviors, process addictions involve compulsion to perform an action despite negative consequences. In this way, people can suffer from dependence on certain processes—they are reliant upon and/or controlled by the addiction as their primary way of dealing with life.

> While the theory about behavioral addictions has been around for a while, only recently have we been able to look at the brain and determine how processes can, in fact, become addictive in the same way as addictive substances. (Grant, et al.)

Exactly which behaviors will be included in this category and put into the *Diagnostic and Statistical Manual* (DSM) is still being debated.

Essentially, what we're doing with process addictions is manipulating our own body chemistry to stimulate or overstimulate pleasure centers of our brain/body. Obviously, we're meant to gain pleasure through our food or engaging in sex, but when we engage compulsively in these behaviors without regard as to negative life consequences or to manage our moods because we're not able to regulate them on our own, they can become addictive in much the same way as any substance can and we no longer have control over them, rather they start to control us. ACAs or those who have experienced childhood trauma can be especially vulnerable to addiction or process/behavioral addictions if they have become emotionally dysregulated through relational trauma.

Sex addiction for example, may be used as a form of mood medication for anxiety, depression, PTSD, or some sex addicts may be reenacting their victimization from childhood sexual abuse, for example, by acting out sexually as adults. If this is the case, they may need to deal with the pain from both their own childhood abuse and the complications caused by their own sexual acting out as an adult, as they recover. As they stop using sex as a form of mood management, they will have to deal with the emotional pain they have been medicating.

In Chapter Thirteen, I include a discussion of "Daily Meds," where we'll talk about how to manipulate your brain/body chemistry in a positive way in order to enhance well-being and self-regulation.

Dark Narcissism: How Deception Hurts the Family

Some of the negative life consequences of process addictions and addiction to drugs and alcohol are what living inside a web of lies does to a family. Years ago, I wrote an article for the *Huffington Post* called "Narcissism in a Bottle." I was surprised by how many people read and responded to the idea, somehow, everyone "got" the thinking behind the title or they wanted to learn more. Self-preoccupation is the very essence of addiction. The deception, first, of the self, and second, of other people, creates a pseudo reality that the whole family is stuck living in. And this isn't true only of addiction to drugs. In fact, addictions to alcohol and drugs are eventually obvious. But some of the behavioral addictions like sex, money addictions or issues (debiting and spending), and food addictions can be surrounded by a complicated web of lies and deceit that throw off everyone's sense of reality. From the point of view of the addict, they are lying about specific things but remain truthful in other areas, so their sense of reality is less undermined than the family's and they don't begin to understand the hurt and havoc that they create through deception and betrayal.

From the point of view of the partner or family, life feels out of control, and the lies feel blindsiding and endless. Not only does the addict lie about what's actually going on in their lives, they lie through making a million little promises that they never keep. And no one else but the person engaged in the hiding knows where the next lie will come from or what the next broken promise will be. So trust is lost, and the burden of reconciliation is placed on the family members who wonder: "Should I forgive again? If I get beyond this one, will I just be setting myself up for being even more hurt next time?"

A couple of things grow out of this. For the family members, deep anxiety and hypervigilance can develop. They are living with so many little untruths that their sense of normal is played with. They walk on eggshells. For the addict, self-preoccupation: "Will they figure it out? Am I still welcome here?" The addict's anxiety can get projected at the family and made about other behaviors that get the focus off of the addiction, "I only act out sexually because I feel unloved. I used to be fine with money. It's our relationship that makes me lie about it; you're scary and controlling."

Here is the narcissism of addiction: because the addict is lying, they become wrapped up in how they are seen, how they are perceived. Then they people-please out of guilt. So rather than a genuine and mature concern for the feelings of the other person, their concern for others stems from their preoccupation with not being found out. And this is one of the ways "normal" can get distorted with both addiction and process addiction. Spouses become deeply hurt and angry, but when they do get mad, they give the addict more to push against, more "reasons" in the addict's mind to justify their behavior. Spouses become controlling because they genuinely cannot trust the person they are partnered with, and life feels so chaotic that they try to put some order into it. Then the addict acts out to "escape the control."

And the family sinks deeper into pain and/or denial. Family members continue to get traumatized and self-medication increases or even spreads. After all, kids imitate their parents, so if Mom or Dad solve their problems by self-medicating and fighting, then "I might as well, too."

When we're locked on a wheel of trauma and addiction, we're self-medicating our trauma, but then, through using substances, we create more trauma. It's a downward spiral. Recovery is about creating an upward spiral—learning how to mood manage and feel good by leaning into recovery supports and healthy habits of meditation, exercise, good nutrition, leisure, and pleasurable activities and relationships. Recovery is also about learning how to sit with pain, breathe through it and process it rather than deaden it. About deciding if it's historical and needs healing, if it's current and can be improved through positive action, if it's something we can fix, or something we need to develop a good attitude about so that we can feel good, even though life isn't perfect.

How Environment Might Create a Desire to Self-Medicate

We have based many of our theories of the addictiveness of drugs on experiments with white rats who were able to push a pedal to

Walking the Wheel of Trauma and Addiction

Prompt: Fill in the blanks.

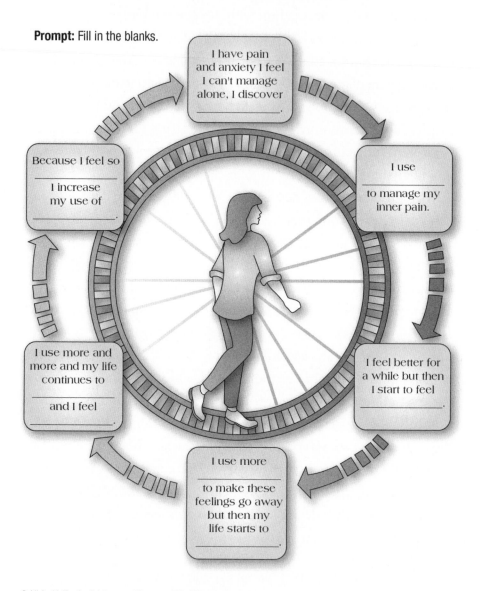

I have pain and anxiety I feel I can't manage alone, I discover _____.

I use _____ to manage my inner pain.

I feel better for a while but then I start to feel _____.

I use more _____ to make these feelings go away but then my life starts to _____.

I use more and more and my life continues to _____ and I feel _____.

Because I feel so _____ I increase my use of _____.

Published in The Soulful Journey of Recovery, *HCI,* © *Tian Dayton, PhD* self-administer morphine. But environment argues Bruce K. Alexander, author of *The Globalization of Addiction,* was not factored into the experiments. Alexander feels that we need to look far beyond our current conventional views to understand what truly drives addiction. Rather than viewing addiction as a disease inside of one person Alexander suggests that we broaden our gaze and begin to examine which elements of the way we live create addiction. He rather skillfully illustrates this point with his experiments on white rats.

During his research on heroin addiction at Simon Fraser University in Vancouver, British Columbia, Canada, Alexander became skeptical of the standardized studies in which rats were kept in small cages with a lever they could press to self-administer morphine or other drugs. The finding from the studies was based on the observation that rats would eventually choose the drug over food. Theories were based on these studies as to the addictiveness of drugs, which made addiction seem almost inevitable. However, Alexander as a social psychologist questioned the set-up of the experiment, noting that the rats, who are basically social animals (think Rat Pack), were under tremendous stress due to the confinement and isolation of these small cages. They felt, in other words, lonely, anxious, and trapped, they felt traumatized by their environment. So he and his research colleagues designed a new experiment, using a different environment that they dubbed, "Rat Park." Unlike the alienation and captivity of a small wire cage, Rat Park was a free-range setup that boasted such amenities as tin cans, running wheels, and wood shavings—all of the things in other words, that might keep a rat happy and relaxed. It also offered soft nests where rats could unwind, curl up, and have a nap or a cuddle.

At Rat Park, when the rats were given the opportunity to self-administer morphine, they tried it but not to excess. They weren't that interested, and they *did not* become addicted. Alexander's findings serve as a counterweight to the prevailing theory that exposure to an overwhelmingly addictive substance automatically creates insatiable cravings for more. In the absence of living environments that created stress and alienation, rats didn't want to self-administer heroin. Having their "creature comforts" well met and leading lives within a network of social support, these rats did not crave relief from outer conditions that created overly stressful inner conditions. They didn't need to use drugs to flee from the emotional and psychological desperation and alienation created by trauma.

How Our Environment Shapes Us

If the community a child grows up in is fairly sustaining and stable, if there are relatives, neighbors, a nice school and faith institution, we can offset some family instability with buffering experiences outside the home. But we have yet to understand the impact of 24-hour news channels and social media on our psyches. And they are tending to take a strong hold just as these other stabilizing forces of family, community and faith institutions are on the decline, they are filling in for what is missing which is exactly a receipt for their becoming a process addiction.

We need real touch not cyber touch to be well adjusted individuals. Before 24-hour news channels came into being, responsible people culled through the events of the day to decide what was important to report on the six o'clock news. Today large companies literally manufacture "news" in order to fill their time and create return on their mega media investments. It is my feeling that this is creating deep anxiety in our culture and rather than making us better informed, is overwhelming and destabilizing us. Much of what gets reported is ramped up so that it can "grab eyeballs" but is often not real news and we don't need to know it. It is designed to create enough anxiety so that we'll want to read on, or stay tuned, the headlines are meant to shock us into interest. This too creates codependency because it makes what is outside of us more important than our own experience of being alive. It makes us worried about our world the way we can worry about our families when they are spinning out of control, it makes the world feel as if it is spinning out of control and just as with dysfunctional families passing down the pain, we start to actually create the experiences that we fear the most. If there were a title for this it might be "When Society Becomes a Dysfunctional Family." The media creates such a powerful sense of connection that it really becomes an extended sense of "family." And we spend a great deal of time with it, sometimes more than our personal relationships.

There are movements countering this phenomenon as was the prediction that John Naisbitt first developed in his 1982 bestseller *Megatrends* where he coined the expression "Hi Tech, Hi Touch." We are as a society developing more Hi Touch experiences like slow eating, self-care, farmer's markets, mindfulness and meditation in order to counter the effects of being constantly pulled out of our inner experience. Only consciousness will be able to overcome unconsciousness and perhaps because the challenges that we face are so much more immediate and threatening to our sense of well-being, so much more "in our face" the solutions we come up with will be more impactful as well.

Light at the End of the Tunnel: Change Conditions from the Start

But it's not all bad news. Harvard University's Center on the Developing Child reports that: "Research also indicates that supportive, responsive relationships with caring adults as early in life as possible can prevent or reverse the damaging effects of toxic stress response." The presence of caring adults who help children to decode the ever-unfolding situations of their worlds is a great protective buffer for the child. Without this reassuring presence, the child has no way of knowing whether or not to be scared or how scared to be, and they have trouble "right-sizing" stressful situations and putting them into a per-spective. They are left instead to come up with their own explanations of events, with limited developmental equipment and support. Stress in the home can also be buffered when kids have access to support or some sort of exit strategy. School, a hobby like sports, afterschool activities, art, or theater, a faith community, youth groups, or simply a nice neighbor that can involve them outside the immediate family, can make all the difference in buffering the effects of toxic stress for a child in a stress filled home.

To deal with what constitutes a national health crisis, Dr. Anda feels we need to reduce the toxic stress load on our developing children. It is very expensive to help people who fall into the healthcare system and the judicial system and improve their outlook once the effects of toxic stress have set in. Much simpler and less expensive is to change our par-enting and educational practices and reduce the effects of toxic stress on the developing child. Rather than wait for diseases to develop and then address them one at a time in adulthood, Anda suggests that we need to look at the child-rearing practices that create the kind of toxic stress that undermines long-term health and resilience (Anda, Felleti, et al., 2006). That kind of toxic stress that pounds away at our autoimmune system in childhood and all too often results in fully developed disor-ders as adults. And it is the kind of toxic stress that becomes modeled and passed down through the generations.

Letter Writing:
Writing a Letter to Your Medicator(s)

Write a letter to whatever form of self-medication you use, whether it be food, starving, cigarettes, liquor, pot, spending/hoarding, drugs, and so on.

Dear _____

_____

_____

_____

_____

_____

_____

_____

_____

_____

_____

_____

_____

_____

_____

_____

_____

_____

_____

_____

_____

_____

_____

_____

_____

_____

_____

_____

_____

❑ Warmly   ❑ Sincerely   ❑ Regretfully   ❑ With relief   ❑ Ambivalently   ❑ Other

CHAPTER TWELVE

Changing the Script: It's Never Too Late to Have a Happy Childhood

"For what it's worth: it's never too late or, in my case,
too early to be whoever you want to be. There's no time limit,
stop whenever you want. You can change or stay the same, there are
no rules to this thing. We can make the best or the worst of it.
I hope you make the best of it. And I hope you see things
that startle you. I hope you feel things you never felt before.
I hope you meet people with a different point of view.
I hope you live a life you're proud of. If you find that you're not,
I hope you have the courage to start all over again."

—Eric Roth, *The Curious Case of Benjamin Button*

When I was about thirty-four years old, I remember standing in the living room of my apartment, looking out the window at Central Park and knowing something wasn't right. I was married to the man I loved, I had two children I adored, and all of the comforts I could want. But I had places inside of me that were numb or still felt just out of reach. I had everything that I wanted. I just wanted to feel it. And some wordy road back to myself was just no good to me. I could

169

see and know what was wrong, I could explain it, and even claim it, but that didn't get me back into those shadowy rooms inside my soul that felt abandoned. Words simply didn't penetrate the silence within me. My family had already worked with Sharon Wegscheider-Cruse and I had gotten a lot out of it. I knew I needed something, so why not try something different—maybe *really* different. And anyway, when you're taking care of two little children anything feels like a vacation, even therapy.

So I arrived for this thing called an experiential something or other after what seemed like an endless drive in a rather pretty area of Pennsylvania. We were doing this at a monastery, so there were lots of Oriental rugs and oak bookshelves. It was lovely and reminded me of the area I grew up in along the city lakes of Minneapolis and the rugs in my childhood living room: heavy, dark, and beautiful. We sat in a big circle and sort of introduced ourselves, which was rather awful. Looking around at the mixture of faces, I decided that there were really only two therapists that I could picture myself working with, but anything else, I felt, would just not be possible; I'd have to fake it. Magically, they were the two I got.

Our therapists led us like third graders into some basement room with pipes along the ceiling that seemed really makeshift. I think we had aluminum folding chairs and a lot of floor pillows and a lot of linoleum. I remember watching a person or two do some sort of psychodrama, a role play where they talked to themselves or their mother or their father or a pillow for that matter. I certainly couldn't see myself doing anything like that in spite of having trained in an acting conservatory. It was just too real, which for me made it too unreal because I had turned off this kind of real somewhere in my teenage years. I had squared my shoulders, summoned the best of me, girded my loins, cleared the decks, pulled myself up by my bootstraps—everything my mom had told me to do. I had put up and shut up and gotten through pretty well, so why in the hell *now*—I mean decades later—was someone telling me it would be worth it for me to go back and revisit this stuff (oh wait a minute; that would be me)? But what was I doing *here*? This was all seeming like maybe a bad idea. I wanted to go home.

"Tian, is there anyone you'd like to talk to?"

"I don't think so; thanks for asking."

"Are you sure? Anyone from your family maybe that you might have something to say to now that you couldn't say then?"

Whaaaa? Was this some kind of seance? Where am I?

"Anyone, just give it a try."

"No, thanks. Thanks ... really, thanks."

"Who, Tian?"

"My dad maybe?"

"Where is he in the room?"

"Over there."

"Big or small?"

"Well both, really."

"Should we put him on a chair?"

"He might fall."

"We'll hold him."

"Go ahead. Knock yourself out."

The sneaky therapists put him on a chair.

Too big, way too big.

So I chose some unsuspecting person to play my beloved, Greek, handsome, dead-drunk dad and proceeded to say some nice, reasonable things to him.

"You were so big to all of us."

"Ahhh.... Is this really you, Dad?"

The next thing I remember was having Kathryn the therapist hold out a red bataka (a large foam bat used in therapy sessions) and ask me if I might like to hit a pillow like so and so had just done.

"Oh no, I don't think so, that's not really my thing, not for me—thanks for thinking of me though." My 1950s lady lessons were flooding my mind with all of the prohibitions against hitting, expressing anger, not smiling, and getting just generally all "turned inside out." This could get out of hand; where is my Kleenex? My bag? When I returned from my torpor, my mental spin through time, she was still standing there, holding the bataka straight up like a padded magic wand or a red cigar. *God, can't she take a hint?*

She held it out again. (My dad smoked cigars, so it was already happening. I was going there, wherever *there* was, feeling a little weird now and on the spot.)

"Do you want to try hitting the pillow once?"

"Maybe *once*, okay! I don't think I can do this, though."

"No problem."

I tried one or two lady-like hits.

"Go on," they encouraged me.

I was caught between not wanting to disappoint them (that just wouldn't be nice) and wanting to run out of the room, up the stairs, into my car, and back home!

"Just let yourself give it a try" *God, they're relentless.*

Then suddenly, all hell broke loose. Like a leopard on the hunt, I pounced on the pillow and hit it over and over and over again.

"Who did you think *you were*? Who did you think *we* were? We're your family, remember us? You were the one big on family all the time.... Where the hell did you go, Dad? Oh Dad, where the hell...did ...you...go? Did you go to hell?"

In a torrent of what now could only be called rage, I went after that red pillow with a vengeance. The nice fifties girl got loose, and in her place was someone for whom this came very easily. Out of the corner of my eye, I saw the man playing Dad reach up and grab the pipes above him and the two therapists grab and steady him, apparently the pillow had moved.

"Excuse me…I'm sorry," I said, thinking I must have just flunked anger work.

"No problem. Keep going, great."

"Great, are you serious? You mean, you're not going to commit me? Well *OOOOKKKKAAAAYYYYY!*"

So, I did. And what I left on the floor that day, on that pillow, in that group was fifteen or twenty years of pain and rage that I had been holding onto without even knowing it. All I knew for sure before coming was that I didn't feel enough of what I knew I could feel, if only I could feel it. And now I was feeling more. And feeling felt really, really good.

Near the end of the week we had a skit night that was absolutely hilarious. Recovery, as it was turning out, was really fun, a little like camp for adults. Someone put music on, and we danced, which research now shows is one of those natural ways of working with trauma. Many cultures have intuitively known this for centuries. Anyway, I just wanted to jump around and literally do high kicks. The energy release I experienced was enormous, and it felt amazing. When I returned from this heart-camp, I found a twelve-step program and started going. And over the next six months or so, I got a therapist and discovered psychodrama, which changed the direction of my career life forever.

Moving Forward: Creating Change

One of the mistakes we can make in recovery is to wait for a fifty-minute appointment once a week to create change. Change is really a daily thing and happens as much or more outside of the therapy room as in it. So when I accept someone into a psychodrama group, I ask them to do several more things. I make sure my clients have a one-to-one therapist because no one can possibly get all of the attention they need and want in group. They need a good one-to-one therapist in order to deconstruct and process all that comes up. I ask them to be in a twelve-step program, any one they identify with. This provides a twenty-four-hour big, beautiful, spiritually alive safety net that is essentially free. It's the foundation of a recovery network from which all else flows.

I talk with them about good exercise habits and eating well. You can gain all the insight in the world, but if you undermine your mental health by ignoring or even abusing your body, you probably won't get better. If they smoke, I ask them to either quit or reduce because if you are smoking, you likely will not grow very much, smoking, like any addiction deadens feeling. Feelings need to be felt both to heal them and to motivate us; feeling is beautiful. I so regret that in this country we have come to pathologize pain. Pain is a part of any life and learning to transform it, to use it as jet fuel to get us to a better place, makes life creative and beautiful. Drug companies would have you think that you need to see a doctor if you've been feeling depressed for more than two weeks. This is cruel to the consumer and makes one think that sadness is wrong or bad and that we need to buy medication from them in order to deal with it. And two weeks of feeling sad is not necessarily cause for alarm, where did we get the idea that if we're not happy, smiling and upbeat at all times something is seriously wrong with us? We get it from advertising, drug companies and social media. Feeling sad sometimes can be perfectly normal. Overdramatizing it, becoming fearful and despondent about feeling down can make things worse. There are many ways to deal with down feelings that involve embracing and processing them and adopting healthy lifestyle changes. Getting involved in something interesting, helping others less fortunate, exercise, healthy distractions, cleaning your closets for that matter are all good choices. One of the great benefits of healing from childhood trauma is the feeling of coming alive again, of finding those shut-down parts, taking ownership and responsibility for them, and welcoming them back into being. Part of that process can hurt, but it's a good hurt because you are coming alive.

Belief in Healing:
Mobilizing the Power of Your Own Mind

Dr. Bruce Lipton, stem cell biologist and bestselling author of *The Biology of Belief,* promotes the idea that your own DNA can be altered and expressed, based on your beliefs. We can use the power of our minds, in other words, to alter our brain chemistry. By *perceiving* the events of our lives in a more positive way, our inner world can become more peaceful. Lipton refers to healing from "the placebo effect," or believing we are being cured or helped by a pill to illustrate the power our minds have to heal us.

A remarkable "one third of all medical intervention is the placebo effect...we didn't get healed by the pill [in other words] we got healed by *the belief in the pill.*" The mind, it turns out, has tremendous power over the body and over how healthy we are.

But the same phenomenon can occur in reverse.

> While the placebo effect refers to the power of the mind to heal us, this ability to think ourselves better actually cuts both ways. We can also think ourselves worse. It's called the *nocebo effect* which refers to the power of our negative beliefs to make us sick. It's equally powerful but in the other direction. If you believe you're going to die you can die from the belief. Thoughts positive or negative shape our biology.

Lipton goes on to suggest that we can use this knowledge to change our lives for the better:

> Now it's time to wake up, because negative thinking is manifesting in negative life experience....95 percent of our lives according to Lipton, comes from our first seven years of unconscious programming as children...so look at the things that come into your life easily. Just look at your life and say where am I struggling?

And once you see that, you can start to understand how you were conditioned to think and begin to make some choices for how you want to continue to think. Do you expect life to be difficult? Do you assume that people will like you once they get to know you? Look at what flows easily into your life both positively and negatively and then see if you can reexamine any negative beliefs and change them for positive ones.

Lipton, who coined the term *epigenetics,* describes that our thoughts have the power to activate our genes. If our genes are a blueprint, our hardware then:

> Epigenetics would be our software. The word "epi" means above. If genes have a role in determining who we are, then *epi*genetic means that something, our beliefs, actually turn on our genes. "Epi" means above, so this is control *above* the genes. In other words, it's our environment and very specifically our *perception* of our environment that can change our genetic activity or the expression of our genes. *How we see who we are, can influence who we become. How we think and feel about ourselves and our lives, can change ourselves and our lives.*

He goes on to describe this phenomenon from the point of view of the person discovering it "so that means . . .

> [I'm] not a victim . . . because I can change my environment and I can change my perception [of my environment], then all of a sudden, if I can do that, then I can control my genes. Then we're going from victim to mastery . . . from genetics to epigenetics.

Albert Einstein echoed just this sentiment in saying that "the world as we have created it is a process of our thinking. It cannot be changed without changing our thinking." Learning to *see* things from a more positive and life-enhancing point of view actually enhances our ability to live a better life and encourages post-traumatic growth. Reframing the events of our lives to see the beauty, meaning, and growth that has taken place, is part of creating emotional health and resilience. "What people have to understand," says Lipton, "is that this doesn't change the genes *it changes the reading and expression of the genes....* So it's not changing the genes it's changing the read-out. A gene is a blueprint... It has no ability to turn itself on and off.... We've been making a big mistake all these years giving it all this power. It's the contractor that we're concerned about (how he reads and builds from the blueprint). It's the mind. Healing yourself is really an adjustment of consciousness not of biology. The brain is the chemist, *change the picture, you change the chemistry.* A gene is a blueprint, not a metric of evolution. What is the metric? Consciousness! Your own DNA can be altered."

Lipton talks about how when we fall in love, the conscious mind is wide awake and we have a heightened awareness of how we feel and behave. We're alert and conscious. But when the "honeymoon" is over, our unconscious programming around relationships takes over. In order to change that unconscious programming, we need to become conscious, to live mindfully, to understand what is going on with us and to then create a daily routine for change.

> Putting a sticky on the refrigerator is like a reminder but it's not a repetition. That's why it doesn't work very well. Repetition is a habit; you have to do something religiously... repeat it and repeat it and repeat it.... to make it a habit.

This is not to say don't use sticky notes; just make sure that you are doing what your sticky note is reminding you to do! "Most change" writes Joe Dispenza in his book, *You Are the Placebo: Making Your Mind Matter*, "starts with the simple process of something outside of us altering something inside of us. If you begin the inward journey and start to change your inner world of thoughts and feelings, it should create an improved state of well-being. If you keep repeating the process in meditation, then in time, epigenetic changes should begin to alter your outer presentation—and you become your own placebo."

Setting My Intention

Answer the following questions for yourself.

1. What I'd like to get from recovery.

_____

_____

_____

_____

2. What I see as the strengths I bring to my recovery are . . .

_____

_____

_____

_____

3. What I see as my weaknesses or growing edge in recovery are . . .

_____

_____

_____

_____

4. What I'd like my life to look like in five years.

_____

_____

_____

_____

CHAPTER THIRTEEN

Packing Your Recovery Suitcase

The way must be in you; the destination also
must be in you and not somewhere else in space or time.
If that kind of self-transformation is being
realized in you, you will arrive.

—Thich Nhat Hanh

You are going on a journey. You will need to adopt and/or develop some qualities that will help you. Here are a few of them.

Humility

If you had to pack your suitcase with certain qualities to take with you on your road to recovery, I would say humility is the first thing to put in. Humility will help you to accept that you may not always be right and that sometimes you need to back up, take a breath, and see things from a different point of view. Humility will help you to be open to learning from others, to see what's out there and who might be able to teach you something. Humility will help you to admit when you are wrong, to apologize, and to repair the inevitable little ruptures that are a part of any relationship.

Courage

You will need courage when it comes to feeling early childhood pain. You will need courage because feeling it can mean falling back into the power imbalance, the innocence, and the vulnerability that were part of the age that pain dates from. You will need courage because you may feel little, helpless, and scared, just as you did then and the fear you felt then may come back. But you will learn to take the hand of that child who lives inside of you, clasp it securely, and walk him or her out of that inner space toward steadier ground. This feeling of being "never understood" is the feeling of your wounded and alone inner child who had no hand to hold when you needed it. *You can change that; you can become your inner child's best grown-up friend.* And only you can do it because only you are there twenty-four hours a day. This is one of those things you need to learn to do for yourself. It's not that you can't lean into someone and open up and ask for company and help; you can. But you have to do the leaning, the asking, the listening, and letting in. You have to, as we say in program, "become willing."

Honesty

As ACAs, we're used to seeing the problem as *out there* and not *within us.* Our many years of false self-functioning and defending against knowing the truth we were living in, can leave a feeling of not wanting to own our side of a problem because when we did that in the past, we just got everything pinned on us. To be upstanding got us nowhere, and others took advantage of it. So, entering recovery and being encouraged to "tell on ourselves" can feel scary, if not just plain stupid. However, it can also be very liberating to clean up on our side of the street, to take responsibility for what we're bringing to the party, because once we do that, we realize that our side of the street is the only thing we could ever clean up anyway. And once we do get honest with ourselves, we can change.

A Good Attitude

Circumstances may not always be under our control but our attitude *is always under our control.* Seeing life from the best perspective possible puts our focus in a positive place. At the very least it can help to counter the impact on ourselves and others of a negative attitude. At the most, it can shape the way we see our lives and the way we frame experience. Reframing is an "attitude adjustment." It can help us to see the events of our childhood in a light that lets them rest more peacefully within us. Thinking of others as doing their best rather than as out to get us for example, can help us to let go of resentment. Seeing the day as pleasant can create more pleasant experiences. Attitude is everything. How you see your life becomes your life.

A Sense of Humor

Don't leave home without this one. Humor is shape shifting. Anyone who has grown up with addiction has probably already got a good sense of humor. Addicts turn reality upside down, humor keeps turning it until, through it's strange alchemy, it lands right-side up again. Humor creates relief. It allows for new points of view. While trauma can make us want to tighten up on controls and become rigid and self-protecting, humor can help to loosen us up. It can give us a sense of control over circumstances. It can reduce the size of a perpetrator or pain in our minds, if we can laugh at them, it loosens their grip on us. Humor is a form of reframing. It is bonding. It has a way of reassuring us that all is not lost, we can still laugh. We can still feel light hearted.

Play, Creativity, and a Sense of Wonder

Make sure you pack these. You will need all of them to restore your sense of fun, play, and aliveness. You will need them to appreciate the mystery of life. We want not simply to survive, we want to thrive, we want to come back to life! The catharsis of laughter is every bit as healing as the catharsis of tears and it pays happy dividends. We need to learn to take ourselves lightly, to laugh, to play, to be easy, and have fun. We need to live this beautiful life we have been given and train ourselves to see beauty in it, not once in a while, but daily.

Mindfulness

If we live in the here and now, we naturally appreciate the moment and all that's in it because we're actually experiencing it rather than racing past it. The moment is, after all, the only place that living is really happening. At the center of mindfulness is learning to witness the inner workings of our own thoughts and emotions, to witness, to watch, and to observe. This skill is fundamental to recovery. When we're in the here and now, what comes up from within is more evident and we see it through calmer and clearer eyes.

Mindfulness is inextricably connected to the breath. Even, rhythmical breathing will allow the nervous system and the mind to calm down. Mindfulness will help you to enjoy a walk, time with a child, or a meal. It will give your mind the ability to focus.

Mindfulness will let you back up from an argument, breathe, take stock, and try a different approach. It will allow you to observe if you are moving toward a panic attack or a rage state.

After an eight-week course in mindfulness, Tom Ireland reports in an article written for *Scientific American*, called "What Does Mindfulness Do for Your Brain?" (June 12, 2014), that these rather startling changes will happen. You will reduce the fight/flight center of your brain, actually shrinking the amygdala. As the amygdala shrinks, the prefrontal cortex thickens (who knew?). The "functional connectivity" between these regions—that is, how often they are activated together—gets weaker, while the connections between areas associated with attention and concentration get stronger.

The implications of this when it comes to trauma resolution are only too obvious. The amygdala, our fear center, down-regulates and sends fewer panic-type messages out to the body and mind, and our thinking mind gets stronger and is better able to hold and process experience and emotion, all of which leads to an enhanced ability to self-regulate. We're getting neurons to fire and wire together in the direction that is more conducive to happy living and calm interactions.

The Basics:
A "Healthy Mind" Platter

Dan Siegel talks about a Healthy Mind Platter that he created with his colleague David Rock:

> What this is, is if you said to yourself "well I'm really wondering what to eat on a daily basis and I put a healthy diet platter right in front of me"... what would the equivalent be for your mind? So there are seven scientifically established activities that actually create a healthy mind, and if you do these every day you're more likely to have health in your life and they're very simple.

> The Healthy Mind Platter has seven essential mental activities necessary for optimum mental health in daily life. These seven daily activities make up the full set of "mental nutrients" that your brain needs to function at its best. By engaging every day in each of these servings, you enable your brain to coordinate and balance its activities, which strengthens your brain's internal connections and your connections with other people.

The seven essential daily mental activities are:

1. **Focus Time.** When we closely focus on tasks in a goal-oriented way, taking on challenges that make deep connections in the brain.

2. **Play Time.** When we allow ourselves to be spontaneous or creative, playfully enjoying novel experiences, which helps make new connections in the brain.

3. **Connecting Time.** When we connect with other people, ideally in person, or take time to appreciate our connection to the natural world around us, richly activating the brain's relational circuitry.

4. **Physical Time.** When we move our bodies, aerobically if possible, which strengthens the brain in many ways.

5. **Time In.** When we quietly reflect internally, focusing on sensations, images, feelings and thoughts, helping to better integrate the brain.

6. **Down Time.** When we are non-focused, without any specific goal, and let our mind wander or simply relax, which helps our brain recharge.

7. **Sleep Time.** When we give the brain the rest it needs to consolidate learning and recover from the experiences of the day.

That you do these things is much more important than *how well* you do them. Habits change through repetition; get there however you can. It's progress, not perfection. Perfection is the enemy of good. Whatever you do, you will always think you could do better. Whatever you finish, you'll always want to add to or tweak. Don't worry about it. Just get started any way you can. Start from where you are right now. Walk or bike to work, take the stairs, meditate while walking, journal on the subway, make a gratitude list in your head, dictate it to your phone, and sing in the shower.

Your Simple Recovery Plan

Addicts, ACAs and ACEs alike, need to actively find new strategies for self-soothing and mood management. We need to work with our body chemistry to create natural and healthy modes of self-regulation. All of the research based activities mentioned below release soothing and self-regulating body chemicals into our blood streams that help us to smooth out our rough edges and feel comfortable and at ease. Following are just some suggestions as to how to garner the effects of these positive mood-altering chemicals. These are the changes that you can begin *today*.

Your Daily Meds

- *Gratitude List.* There is so much research on how well this works that it's just pointless not to do it. So make a list of the things in your life right now, at this moment, that you are grateful for and appreciate. It can be as simple as a soft pillow and a cup of tea or coffee in the morning. Or it could be gratitude for those you love, your pet, your job, your health, and so on. Whatever it is, the feeling of gratitude and appreciation literally has the power to communicate with the cells of your body and change them. And it will positively impact the quality of your day.
- *Recovery Journal.* Journaling elevates the immune system according to Dr. James Pennebaker of the University of Texas. Pennebaker recommends journaling for about twenty minutes, then taking a break and if you want to journal more, go back to it. From a trauma perspective journaling integrates thought and feeling. It strengthens your inner witness. Journaling helps your thinking mind to make meaning out of the feelings and sense memories that may not be fully in your conscious awareness. Journaling not only releases soothing dopamine into our bodies,

it can actually help them to heal faster, reports Elizabeth Broad-
bent, professor of medicine at the University of Auckland in
New Zealand, in a study published in July 2013 in *Psychosomatic
Medicine*. A surprising 76 percent of adults in the "journaling
group" were fully healed eleven days after getting a biopsy procedure, while in contrast, only 58 percent of the control group
who did not journal had not recovered at that same point. This
"faster healing" group got their 18 percent jump on healing by
journaling for twenty minutes on three consecutive days two
weeks before their procedure. The study concluded that writing
about their distressing thoughts and feelings for even one hour,
was able to help those participating to make sense of events and
reduce distress, which resulted in their bodies healing much
faster than those who did not have this expressive outlet.

- *Exercise.* Walking in nature or with friends, gives us a serotonin
  blast that is self-regulating and can be as effective as medication
  in treating depression. We can "dose" ourselves with a brisk
  walk three or four times a week for around forty-five minutes.
  Studies conducted in Sweden and at Duke University found
  that walking works as well as medication in treating depression.
  In fact, it can work better as there are no side effects and there
  is no need to come off of meds. There is also enhanced fitness
  and a sense of personal agency that this approach to working
  with depression creates.

- *Healthy Eating.* You can't look in your inbox, pick up a paper or
  a magazine without encountering information on good nutrition. This is crucial. A healthy, sensible diet will give you what
  your body needs to stay balanced, and it's an important part of
  self-regulation. We know that smoking, drinking, and drugging
  create addiction. We can also become addicted to sugar, white
  flour, and junk food; these foods set up cravings and high/low

cycles in the body that interfere with healthy self-regulation. If you want to become emotionally healthy, you will need to build healthy eating and exercise into your life.

- *Inspiration.* You can do this through meditation, inspiring readings, guided meditations or guided imageries (see *tiandayton. com/soulfuljourney*), or listening to something that motivates or stirs you. Inspiration helps to keep the brain fit and young. Guard your meditative/quiet/reflective time, even if it's ten minutes on the subway, bus, on a walk, or listening to uplifting and inspiring books on tape as you make your way to work or go on errands.

Network Your Healing

Relationships not only soothe our bodies, they are core to our sense of well-being. People with a relationship network live longer and healthier lives according to Harvard researchers. "Social connections...not only give us pleasure, they also influence our long-term health in ways every bit as powerful as adequate sleep, a good diet, and not smoking. Dozens of studies have shown that people who have satisfying relationships with family, friends, and their community are happier, have fewer health problems, and live longer. Conversely, a relative lack of social ties is associated with depression and later-life cognitive decline, as well as with increased mortality. One study, which examined data from more than 309,000 people, found that lack of strong relationships increased the risk of premature death from all causes by 50 percent—an effect on mortality risk roughly comparable to smoking up to fifteen cigarettes a day, and greater than obesity and physical inactivity." (*Strengthen Relationships for Longer, Healthier Life*, Harvard Health Publishing 2010.) If we have been hurt in relationships, then relationships are our path to healing!

Recover-Me-Time

Twelve-Step Meetings. Twelve-step meetings can be the core of your recovery. What's important is that you familiarize yourself with the principals of the program and that you find "rooms" of people who are on a recovery journey like you are. Meetings I find are regional. For example, in some areas of the country or world the same meeting, say Al-Anon or CODA or ACA meetings will be different according to where they are. Go to the meetings that feel right to you and are best in your area. Find the meetings that suit you and the issues you're dealing with. There are meetings for Alcoholics Anonymous (AA), Drug Addicts Anonymous (DAA), Overeaters Anonymous (eating disorders, OA), family members of addicts (Al-Anon), Debtors Anonymous (DA), Sex Addicts Anonymous (SAA), Codependents Anonymous (CoDA), and Adult Children of Alcoholics/Dysfunctional Families (ACA) and others just a Google search away. My personal suggestion would also be to consider starting Emotional Sobriety Anonyomous (ESA) meetings.

Therapy Basics

Group Therapy: Group therapy is rather remarkable, you can spin your wheels thinking about recovery, and sometimes one-to-one can move slowly but groups will stimulate relational healing. I have a strong preference for psychodrama groups for trauma resolution, but groups in general are just a great way to simulate, practice, and consolidate gains in relational healing.

One-to-One Therapy: At some point one-to-one therapy can feel very supportive. No group can give you the one-to-one attention to deconstruct all of the feelings that groups mobilize, but one-to-one therapy once or twice a week can.

Recovery Weeks. There are five-day experiential programs, like the ones I designed for The Meadows Rio Retreat, Thrive—Going to the

Next Level, and Mending Heartwounds that can really support and renew your recovery and/or grief process. They help to get you on or revitalize your path of healing. The combination of small group support with like-minded people and professional support, research-based learning and experiential therapy is very powerful. Because they are generally about five days, they fit into your life and you can return home refreshed and motivated to make changes. I love these programs for our population because you can carve out time in your life just for you, I even feel that they can create a sort of peak experience in healing as I discuss in our last chapter.

Your Online Interface with Soulful Journey. Log onto *tiandayton. com/soulfuljourney*, for lots of extra oomph in the form of meditations, guided imageries, inspiring videos, and articles. You will also find my online, interactive, and playful system for processing emotions called "emotionexplorer." These are there to support your recovery process and to provide a multi-sensory, online experience. At the end of the book, I have suggestions on how you can start your own peer support group.

Think of today as simply another day on your journey of recovery, or your spiritual journey—or however you like to frame it. Because we take this journey a day at a time, the fewer preconceived notions we have about how it should be, or where we should be at any given moment, the better. Be sure to have fun. We are funny people; we're creative, ingenious, and smart. Our graveyard humor is hilarious. Along with letting go of lots of unshed tears, you should find yourself doubled over with laughter over and over again along this soulful journey. Enjoy the ride.

Exercise:
The Trauma Timeline

I developed The Trauma Timeline late in the 1980s and first published it in my book *The Living Stage*. It has become an industry standard. The version I have found most impactful is to simply list traumas and to have a separate timeline for breakthroughs (*tiandayton.com /soulful journey*). I have done The Trauma Timeline in groups, at conferences, in treatment centers, inpatient programs, in outpatient programs, in prison programs, and more. The two spontaneous awareness's most stated by participants have been "I didn't realize that traumas in my life were centralized mostly in this part of my life. It felt as if everything was traumatic because we never talked about anything in our family, it was all so hidden." And another common observation goes something like this, "I see how I have been living out these trauma relational dynamics and recreating them throughout my life." A third has been an awareness that someone wants to reconnect with their carefree self, oftentimes a childhood self, perhaps before they felt burdened by problems.

The Trauma Timeline

In the area on the following page that corresponds to the appropriate year, just jot down any traumas, losses, or painful times of your life that you feel hurt you.

90 yrs ————————————

————————————— 85 yrs

80 yrs ————————————

————————————— 75 yrs

70 yrs ————————————

————————————— 65 yrs

60 yrs ————————————

————————————— 55 yrs

50 yrs ————————————

————————————— 45 yrs

40 yrs ————————————

————————————— 35 yrs

30 yrs ————————————

————————————— 25 yrs

20 yrs ————————————

————————————— 15 yrs

10 yrs ————————————

————————————— 5 yrs

0 yrs ————————————

Trauma Timeline™, © Tian Dayton, PhD, TEP

The Trauma Timeline
Journaling Exercise

Answer the following questions:

1. What pops out as significant when you look at your Trauma Timeline? Please describe.

_____

_____

_____

_____

2. What periods of your life seemed to have the most difficult times? Please describe.

_____

_____

_____

_____

3. What periods in your life seemed relatively calm? Please describe.

_____

_____

_____

_____

4. Are there moments when it felt like everything changed for the worse? Please describe.

_____

_____
_____
_____

5. Are there moments when it felt like everything changed for the better? Please describe.

_____
_____
_____
_____

6. Do you see patterns or dynamics from your childhood that you repeated in your adult relationships?

_____
_____
_____
_____

7. What would you like to say to yourself at any point along your Trauma Timeline from where you are today? Please identify the time and say it.

_____
_____
_____
_____

8. What strengths do you feel you developed through dealing with these life issues? Please describe.

_____
_____
_____
_____

CHAPTER FOURTEEN

Grief Work: Spinning Straw into Gold

Death is not the greatest loss in life.
The greatest loss is what dies inside us, while we live.

—Norman Cousins

W hen I was around twenty-three, I dragged my family (of origin) to a few sessions of therapy. After being with us for a while the therapist said, "This family needs a funeral." And he was right. My father, in fact, had just died and we of course did have a funeral for him, a sad one. But we were no longer a family who could grieve normally together. We needed a different kind or ritual because, in truth, we had lost him years before that. We had lost him to addiction and along with that we had lost the family as we knew it. Because of the trauma surrounding our parents' sudden (as far as I knew anyway) divorce, Dad's addictions both to alcohol and to sex and because we grew up at a time when all of this was not very well understood and covered in shame and silence, we lost things that at the time didn't even have a name. And along with it, a part of ourselves and an easy access to each other. We were very connected, but there was an elephant in the living room that no one could quiet step around. And every time we bumped into it, there was a muffled roar that seemed to feel like it was coming out

195

of nowhere. And the longer we didn't talk about the real pain, the more the pain started to wear different names, it got made about whoever was triggering it. But it was at the wrong time, in the wrong place, and over the wrong thing. But back then we didn't know any of that.

Funerals are incredibly helpful for honoring the death and the life of a person we have lost. They offer a structure through which to legitimize loss and to grieve—to actually feel the pain we're in.

But there are no ceremonies for the child who loses a parent slowly to the disease of addiction. Or the traumatized individual who has lost a connection with themselves. There are simply no rituals for these. No black armbands to let the world know that we're hurting. No casseroles are dropped off to keep us fed until we can get on our feet again. And no one honors the addict who only sort of died, or us for losing them by inches, or notices the part of us that died a little, too.

Besides, we would need two eulogies. One the classic going over of his life, his strengths, contributions and those he left behind who will mourn him. That one is very important and healing. But there is a shadow eulogy that never gets said because it happens long before the real death.

"This man is dying while he is living, and he is taking a part of us along with him."

Or my husband's mother. "This mother is no longer able to be who she was; she is somewhere we cannot find her. And she can no longer find herself."

At my father's funeral, I hung onto the Greek priest's words, repeated many times: "number him among the just." They gave me peace. I thought my father deserved them (although I did appreciate the priest making it official). It was so painful to see addiction take away the love and respect from him that he had earned for most of his life. So my mourning wasn't only for me, I needed to also mourn what I witnessed my father losing, which I think is the case for many of us who watch our parent sink into addiction and never come out of it.

When addiction robs us of someone we love whether a child, parent, sister, brother or partner and also undermines that person in the eyes of the community we live in, it just becomes a deep, complicated, and throbbing ache that we don't know what to do with. And there is no healthy reminiscing of what we *did* have. No linking of arms and pulling together to support each other through the pain and to hold onto our good memories. As identified by our therapist, my family needed to mourn the family we had lost so that we could pull together and be the family we could still be.

We lose an addict over and over and over again to their substance, which means that we suffer a rupture over and over again. We hope over and over again. We trust over and over again, and our trust is violated over and over again. This is much more complicated than losing someone once. And the feelings aren't simple. We feel guilt, both of what we could perhaps have done or didn't do, or survival guilt: why are we okay when they aren't? Or we experience guilt for wishing them out of our lives. We feel freaked out at having such a close brush with darkness, with mental illness. We feel anger and disappointment, and we feel loss— terrible, searing loss—of someone who went too soon and too horribly.

And one other thing we ACAs grieve is what never got a chance to happen: our unlived life as a child.

When we can't mourn, for whatever reason, we're left feeling haunted by memories we don't know what to do with. If we don't do something to work through them, they remain with us. Untethered to time and place, they float around, unwelcome intruders—but not gone. And decades later, we are still warding off ghosts from the past and hurt that was never acknowledged; we are still mystified. We clutch the scattered scraps of a life we once had as proof, evidence that it was really there. And we try to forget what we can't quite remember.

Relational trauma needs to be grieved. When it is not, we are left wandering through the rooms and corridors of our youth, looking for ourselves, our parents, our families, looking for the life we lost. We're confused by the way we had to go underground to save our sense of self. We lose connection to parts of us that died or feigned death in order to remain strangely living. If we do not locate and feel these disowned parts of self, if we do not visit the corners of our mind and heart that have subsisted, folded in on themselves and tucked away from daylight, we will not become whole. And we will not feel fully alive. Grief allows our hearts to breathe.

What hurt us most is often what we hide from the most. As adult children, if we don't get some healing around our trauma, we never really leave our families. We stay stuck in a time and space from the past, a period in our lives that hurt us the most, so much in fact, that we cannot bear to "go there." It hangs lost and still, frozen in space, and a part of us is frozen along with it.

Hidden and Disenfranchised Losses

Some losses like death are clear. Society recognizes them as significant and we have rituals to mourn them. We feel free to ask for support and more often, support comes our way without our even having to ask. But the kinds of losses that surround relational trauma and addiction are not necessarily acknowledged and they do not necessarily get grieved. Because of this they often remain what is referred to as "disenfranchised." Disenfranchised losses can lack visibility and clarity. They are split out of consciousness and oftentimes remain unseen or misread by others and even by ourselves. There can even be confusion as to exactly who or what has been lost or whether there is a loss at all. However, not only do these losses exist, the very fact that they remain buried and unrecognized can create blocks in our process of grieving and recovery. These sorts of losses need our compassion and care. Grieving these kinds of losses can bring about change on the inside, that leads to change on the outside.

Some examples of disenfranchised losses are:

- Loss of a connection to self, due to trauma
- The grief of the *inner child* who lives inside of the adult
- For the addict, the loss of potential or a part of their life
- For the ACA, the loss of a sober parent or a period of unencumbered childhood
- For the ACA, the loss of a functional family
- For the spouse of an addict, the loss of a trusted and dependable partner
- Divorce abandonment/visitation changes related to divorce
- Socially stigmatized deaths (AIDS, suicide, murder, DUI, overdose, death)
- Adoption either being adopted or placing a child up for adoption, adoptive parents whose child seeks a biological family
- Death of a pet
- Miscarriage, infertility
- Disabling conditions, health issues
- Moving to a new home, job loss, retirement
- Mental illness or cognitive deficit

Mourning a loss of a connection to self or to someone significant, to the sober parent, to a period of life, to family addiction and/or dysfunction is as crucial as mourning a loss to death. Processing these losses experientially provides an alternative form of ritual for the kinds of losses that all too often go unrecognized and unacknowledged. People often feel alone in grieving this kind of loss, but being with a small group of individuals as you are at Mending Heartwounds, who are also looking at and dealing with them, can give a sense of permission and freedom in facing them. And concretizing can give them a sense of being real.

I think that psychodrama can be used to create what I call "Life Rituals." As our life span increases, we need rituals to honor passages such as sobriety, divorce, retirement, empty nest and inner child work.

THE MANY FACES OF GRIEF

Grief is a mosaic of different feelings. Some feelings are frozen, lost or thrown away. Anger, rage, sorrow, yearning, desperation, loneliness, and oddly enough, even a kind of ecstasy can all be a part of deep grief. Perhaps this is why grieving is so liberating; it springs us loose of feeling trapped in our own, unfelt emotions and it puts us in touch with our deeper essence.

Grief can hide behind many masks and can pop out in numerous and sometimes surprising disguises. Among them are:

- Sudden angry outbursts
- Rage
- Excessive rumination
- Chronic negativity
- Being easily triggered/overly intense emotional reactions
- Recurring or long-lasting depression
- Chronic anxiety
- Self-mutilation and self-harming
- Caretaking behavior
- Excessive guilt
- Constant crying or feeling weepy
- Low mood, sad
- Excessive anxiety
- Emotional numbness or constriction
- Shame
- Codependency
- Body issues/health related, soreness, stiffness
- A desire to self-medicate

Recognizing some of the feelings/behaviors listed above as connected to unresolved grief provides a way of dealing with them. Passing through the pain that has been the driver behind self-destructive behaviors, really entering into a grief process for the part of self who needs to mourn, or the wounded inner child/adolescent or young adult, is deeply freeing and healing. It is necessary.

The Grief of the Inner Child

One of the problematic issues for adult children is that some if not much of their mourning dates from a time and place in their childhood. Many of them feel too old to let themselves exhibit the kind of grief they actually feel. Some have parents who are now sober with whom they have vastly improved relationships. They don't want to jeopardize their relationship today by releasing their pain, but it still needs to be felt and processed because they still carry it and perhaps live it out. It becomes important for these adult children to actually *speak from the role of their inner child to the parent they had then.*

An adult child might find themselves in a bind. While finally getting what they always wanted, a sober parent and a comfortable relationship with them, the child inside may still be in pain; they may still need to cry and get angry.

The ACA loves their now-sober parent, and their now-sober parent likely wants to forget about all of those terrible years, at least the half they don't remember anyway. They want to make their amends and have it over with. But for the ACA, it is far from over, and now they are faced with the complicated task of loving their sober parent while still needing to confront the parent they grew up with. They need to grieve that parent, to get angry at that parent, to call that parent onto the carpet, and tell them how much they have been hurt by them. But they're afraid to because they got what they always wanted, which is a sober parent. And they, too, want to forget; they don't want to rock the boat. However, out of sight is not out of mind. The average ACA will need to grieve these losses to get over them.

It is such a shame that we avoid grief because, truthfully, it's the fastest way through what blocks our joy. And when I say fast, I mean it; if you really let yourself feel pain, you will cry, get angry, feel tossed around, disequilibrated a bit and also freed up, relieved, and even exhilarated. And all of this can happen in twenty minutes. It comes in waves. And each wave brings another layer of healing along with it. Don't resist it, don't get stuck in it, and you'll see great results. One of the things that can complicate mourning is if there are piled up, ungrieved losses from the past that interfere with our grieving a loss in the present. When this is the case, the current loss gets confused with past losses and we feel overwhelmed, then we may want to shut the door on the whole thing. Gaining some clarity around these kinds of losses helps us to separate the past from the present. Then we can see the losses more clearly and give them the airtime that they need and deserve. Then we can move through our grief and loss toward renewal and reinvestment. Fill in the blanks on the chart on the next page with memories of losses from the past that a current loss might be triggering.

Getting Loose of Trauma Bonds: Separating Past from Present

We move through the world in the present, but carrying the past. In order to relieve ourselves of the weight of unfelt, unprocessed emotion, our inner world needs to somehow be made manifest. It needs to come out, and psychodrama makes that very easy because it allows for the full and, if desired, cathartic expression of whatever emotions are in there. It lets us express our sadness or anger to the actual person toward whom we feel it through role players. It can be so unsatisfying, to say nothing of detrimental, to express historical pain that is tied to our drunk mother when we were thirteen, as a forty-year-old to that same mother who may be sober. They may have forgotten about what we're talking about or may not want to hear it. But role play allows those historical periods of our lives to come alive for a moment, and we can go full throttle into our grief and anger. The satisfaction, the release, and the freedom can be profound. Because we're re-inhabiting that

Loss Chart

Prompt: Fill in the blanks.

thirteen-year-old and letting her or him speak to the right person at the right time through surrogates. The thirteen-year old *can talk, through using role players, to the parent they had then, the one that hurt them.* We can leave the relationship with the mother we have today out of it and address historical issues on the therapeutic stage. It's so much truer and curiously feels more real and it certainly creates less wear and tear on the relationship today that may be working well.

The ACA loves their now-sober parent, and their now-sober parent likely wants to forget about all of those terrible years, at least the half they don't remember anyway. They want to make their amends and have it over with. But for the ACA, it is far from over, and now they are faced with the complicated task of loving their sober parent while still needing to confront the parent they grew up with. They need to grieve that parent, to get angry at that parent, to call that parent onto the carpet, and tell them how much they have been hurt by them. But they're afraid to because they got what they always wanted, which is a sober parent. And they, too, want to forget; they don't want to rock the boat. However, out of sight is not out of mind. The average ACA will need to grieve these losses to get over them.

One of the things I try to teach clients how to do is to allow the child or wounded part within them to talk to their "inner adult" before blurting out all of their feelings to the world and then being disappointed that the world doesn't hear, care, or listen. It is our job to hear ourselves as adults, to be our own good parent, to listen to all that the various parts of ourselves are trying to say to us. Then, to help find the right words for the right feeling so that we have a chance to communicate our feelings with some level of awareness, compassion and emotional intelligence. When we can do this, we have a pretty good shot at being understood. And when we can listen as someone else attempts to do the same with us, we have the basis for intimacy and success in relationships, whether with friends, or in the workplace. Naturally, we'll have our angry outbursts, our tears, frustrations, and momentary wobbles, but they need to be temporary; we need to find our way back to forgiveness, understanding, and communication.

It is such a shame that we avoid grief because, truthfully, it's the fastest way through what blocks our joy. And when I say *fast*, I mean it; if you really let yourself feel pain, you will cry, get angry, feel tossed around, dis-equilibrated a bit and also freed up, relieved, and even exhilarated. And all of this can happen in twenty minutes. It comes in waves. Don't resist it, don't get stuck in it, and you'll see great results.

Psychodrama makes this sort of dynamic much clearer than words ever could. It takes you directly to the moment in time where a painful complex got set up and creates an in vivo moment to revisit, relive, and release, or as J. L. Moreno said, to "do, undo, and redo."

Here's an example of how that might look. Imagine that a client has been sharing about what she carries from the past about her father but is only marginally aware of how or why.

I might say, "Would you like to choose someone to play your sober dad today? We'll keep Dad and your current relationship with him over here, safe. Now choose someone to play Dad when he was drunk or high or abusive, so you can deal with him, okay? And I promise, we won't tell Dad you are doing this. It's just for you, so have at it." I try to reassure her that we won't touch what's working, that she is fully entitled to protect this dad she is now so close to, and we can then deal with the dad she had in childhood in order to heal her "inner child," her "inner adolescent," or whatever inner part of her that needs attention.

And clients aren't going there alone; I am with them as is the group, supporting them, helping them through, and keeping things safe. One way that you can approximate this experience on your own is to write a letter, not to be sent, to the part of yourself, another person, a time of life, or a circumstance that you're saying goodbye to, grieving for or want to work with. When you write it for your eyes only, you can fully express your feelings, and say everything you need or long to say. Let the paper listen to you, and let yourself talk. You may be surprised at how good it feels. Once you finish the letter, you can decide what to do with it. If you want to share it in therapy or with a trusted friend or support group, you can. Or, you can do something to ritualize the letting go process by burying it in nature, putting it somewhere, or tearing it up. It is simply a vehicle for self-expression and not written to be sent to anyone at all.

Stages of Grief and Mourning from Relationship Trauma

Stages of Grief and Mourning	Emotional Feelings and Manifestations	Psychological Ideations and Manifestations	Behavioral Actions Manifestations	Physiological Sensations and Manifestations	Healing Manifestations
Numbness/ Shutdown and Frozeness	Low affect/Limited feeling palate/Emotional Constriction/Shame/ Feeling lost and unmoored.	Denial/Dissociation/ Splitting/Rewriting reality to make it palatable/ Avoidance of pain.	Enervation, low activity level/ Trouble focusing and attending/Self-medication/ Isolation or withdrawal.	Body issues/Back pain, muscle stiffness, muscle or body soreness/Low energy/Trouble mobilizing.	Getting in touch with sadness and anger/Relief in allowing feelings to flow/ Increased energy.
Yearning and Searching	Anxiety/Feeling Lost/ Sense of emptiness/ Yearning for what was lost/Searching for a replacement/Rumination.	Difficulty focusing and organizing time/Free floating or general-ized anxiety/Regret, bargaining.	Ups and downs/Reach-ing out and pulling back/ False starts/Looking for direction from others.	Head pounding/Stomach queasiness/Tingling or tightness in chest, neck, jaw, shoulders.	Reaching out to others/ Taking in support, caring, advice/Sense of hope that things will get better.
Disorganization Anger and Despair	Low mood/Avoidant/Guilt/ Sadness/Anxiety/ Negative inner mono-logue/Bouts of sadness/ Feeling lost/hopeless.	Recurring or long lasting depression/Rumination, negativity/Difficulty focus-ing and organizing time/ strained relationships	Sudden angry outbursts/ Rage/Teary, crying/Abuse of others/Self-harming/ Self-sabotage/Bullying/ Complaining/Stonewalling.	Heart racing, tightness in chest/Shortness of breath/Increased blood or adrenaline flow/Low energy.	Increased emotional mod-ulation/ Lighter, more even mood/Mind fogginess clearing/Less anxiety/More engagement with others.
Acceptance Integration and Reorganization	Even mood/Sense of inner peace/present in the moment/Reality-oriented/greater calm and contentment/Emo-tional regulation and sobriety.	Greater ability to focus and follow through/ Greater ease/Lessening of debilitating or negative thinking/Greater positiv-ity/Life engagement.	Engagement in social activities/Self-care/ Engagement in leisure and fun activities/ More able to find meaning in work and/or activities.	More even breathing, more energy/Greater heart and body coherence/ Greater sense of physical relaxation/Greater body-mind integration.	Positive self-esteem start-ing to return/An ability to feel internally organized/ Life feels more meaning-ful and purposeful/More satisfying connectedness with others.
Reinvestment/ Renewal	Renewed energy for life/A healthier feeling about the self, increased sense of satisfaction, excite-ment and energy for life.	Greater focus/Imagina-tion and creative think-ing/Deepened capacity for appreciation, joy and intimacy	New relationships/Rein-vesting in life activities and relationships/New endeavors/Flow and fun activities	More energy, even breath-ing, a feeling of get up and go, body awareness, greater sense of well being/ Healthier habits.	Post-traumatic growth/ Awareness of a broader self/A sense of wonder and mystery/Altruism, compassion, spirituality.

Tian Dayton PhD TEP. Permission to reprint granted with the following attribution. First published in The Soulful Journey of Recovery, Health Communications, Inc. 2019

Body Manifestations of
Grief and Mourning Reflections

1. Which stage of the mourning process do you identify with at this moment if any? Please say why.

_____

_____

_____

_____

_____

_____

2. How do the manifestations of this stage appear for you?

   A. Emotional _____

_____

_____

_____

_____

   B. Psychological _____

_____

_____

_____

_____

C. Behavioral _____

_____

_____

_____

_____

_____

D. Physiological _____

_____

_____

_____

_____

_____

E.Healing _____

_____

_____

_____

_____

_____

CHAPTER FIFTEEN

Finding Forgiveness: Your Get-Out-of-Jail-Free Card

"We must develop and maintain the capacity to forgive.
He who is devoid of the power to forgive is devoid of the power
to love. There is some good in the worst of us and some
evil in the best of us. When we discover this, we are
less prone to hate our enemies."

—Martin Luther King Jr.

I n the 1980s, I wrote *Forgiving and Moving On*. The publisher said, "We need to change the title; research shows that people don't buy books on forgiveness." At this point in time, forgiveness wasn't being talked about in the mental health field; it was seen as the province of religion. As hard as we tried, we couldn't find another title that reflected the contents of the book, which was essentially daily readings that dealt with the feelings and thoughts that come up around letting go, forgiving, and moving on. We decided to go ahead with the title we had, and, it became a recovery best seller.

Forgiveness is a process, not an event. It takes time and work to plow through the anger, resentment, and hurt that are often in the way.

Because it's a process, it doesn't need to happen all at once. Forgiveness can free us from the soul-eating pain of living with rancor and resentment whether or not we wish to continue a relationship with the person we're forgiving. Far from being a way to whitewash a circumstance, forgiveness implies that there is fully something that happened that is difficult enough to overlook or live with, that it actually requires forgiveness. The same is true with forgiving ourselves, it benefits no one for us to carry hatred and recrimination towards ourselves, it just makes us less present for healthy relating in the present and it blocks our recovery. Self-forgiveness takes humility because we are taking an honest self-inventory. We're willing to live with the truth of our own actions while simultaneously making a commitment to change our behavior. It takes character.

I learned to forgive because I saw it as my only way out of the kind of chronic emotional and psychological pain that inevitably surrounds addiction. It felt like self-love. My goal was to move on as unscathed as possible. It is not up to me to mete out punishment, nor do I enjoy doing that. If I spend all of my time figuring out what another person "deserves," I drain my energy and use it up on them and stay stuck, right alongside them. It's living in a negative frame and unintelligent in my eyes. This for me means that forgiveness is always the right solution, that the point is to forgive *until I am free*, until my spirit is released, to live freely in this beautiful and abundant world and allow my energy to be deployed in the directions of my choosing, not determined by someone else's bad actions. So forgiveness in this sense, feels intelligently selfish.

Once you get into recovery, you start to realize that maybe you're not the problem after all. You begin to identify the forces that victimized you within the family dynamic. You get angry, sad, disappointed, and you feel your years of hurt. And the therapeutic community cheers you on for "getting in touch with your feelings," and that can feel vindicating. While this is a crucial part of healing, it can morph into being stuck in blame and not taking responsibility for moving beyond it. Forgiveness helps us to get over that hump.

Forgiveness Myths: What Blocks My Ability to Forgive?

If we forgive it doesn't mean we have to eradicate any residual feelings of hurt and anger or we haven't really forgiven. That's too high a bar. I see forgiveness as heading in the right direction, so that if vengeful thoughts start to overtake us, we can check in with ourselves and renew our decision to move past them.

Forgiveness is a recognition within the self of a wish or a need to place a particular issue into a different internal context; moving something from the foreground to the background. When we consider forgiveness as part of our healing process, we're recognizing that we want inner peace more than a grudge to nurse. We're forgiving to free ourselves and to restore our own equilibrium and sense of joy. It is a statement about where we are in our own healing process.

There are a few stumbling blocks when people I work with consider forgiveness. One is the feeling that if they forgive, they are in some way condoning wrong actions. Another is the finality of it and releasing the hope of ever righting the wrong or getting retribution. Another is letting go of the wish of finally getting what they always wanted. Still another is the implication that forgiveness means that they wish to continue having a relationship with the person they're forgiving. But forgiving someone who has hurt us, doesn't necessarily mean we want to continue a relationship with him or her. Forgiveness is not a one-time event and it doesn't mean we relinquish our right to continued feelings about an issue.

When I began working with clients, addressing forgiveness issues experientially, the things that people struggled with became evident.

And they really struggled. I found that it was hard for people to talk about forgiveness, but they could relate to what I called "myths" or blocks. And they found it liberating to talk about those. Eventually once I developed "Floor Checks," I just put them all around the floor and I'd ask a series of questions, like "Which myth do you feel drawn to now? Walk over to it, stand next to it, and share about why you chose it." What came out of people was magical, as it always is. Case studies on what kinds of feelings came up around considering forgiveness started appearing all around the room, for everyone to share and identify with. And the rest just happened, the interaction of the group took over and an experience materialized.

Here are the myths surrounding forgiveness as I see them:

- If I forgive, my relationship with the person I'm forgiving will definitely improve.
- If I forgive, I'll no longer feel angry at that person for what happened.
- Forgiving myself is selfish.
- If I forgive, I forego my right to hurt feelings.
- If I forgive, it means I want to continue to have a relationship with the person I'm forgiving.
- If I forgive, it means I'm condoning the behavior of the person I'm forgiving.
- If I haven't forgotten, I haven't really forgiven.
- I only need to forgive once.
- I forgive for the sake of the other person.

Myths Around the Idea of Forgiveness

Using numbers from 1–10 rate how much you feel each of these myths is at play in your life. Then jot down a few feeling words that come to mind when you look at each one.

Making Amends (Working the Ninth Step)

Addicts or people who have hurt their families or children can carry a deep sense of self-loathing for their actions. They need to do what they can to make it right, if the situation permits, so that they take responsibility for their own behavior. Otherwise they risk feeling very bad about themselves, plagued with guilt, shame and other negative feelings that can make them want to self-medicate to make the pain go away—to relapse, in other words. Or their lack of amends leaves a person who has caused pain in a sort of gray zone, they haven't asked for forgiveness, been willing to hear how they have hurt someone and commit to a change in behavior. They haven't owned and cleaned up their side of the street. The Twelve Steps stress the importance of addicts making amends in order to stay sober, both physically and emotionally. ACAs or anyone who has caused another pain can work this same step if we feel a need to, remember there are many ways to self-medicate and there are many ways to act out and pass on pain.

Addictive or acting out behaviors are often attempts at running from our own inner turbulence, misguided efforts at quieting an inner storm. The storm is often about feeling hurt by others or hurting others through our own behavior. The two are intertwined, feeding and fueling off each other. Asking for or granting forgiveness offers a way out, a way to make an attempt at restitution, to restore peace and serenity. We've done our part to right a wrong.

Dr. Ken Hart of the Leeds Forgiveness for Addiction Treatment Study (FATS) says, "Controversy often arises because people fail to understand that forgiveness is always desirable, but attempts at reconciliation may sometimes be ill-advised." Dr. Hart's study is testing two different approaches to forgiveness: *secular* and *spiritual.*

The secular approach aims to speed up the growth of *empathy* and *compassion* so that addicts can better understand the imperfections and flaws of those who have hurt them. In psychodrama, we do this through role reversal by giving clients the opportunity to stand in the shoes of another person. Usually, they come to realize that the sense of "badness" they carry around from having interpreted their abuse to mean "something must be wrong with me or I wouldn't be treated this way," isn't and probably was never true. They were in the wrong place at the wrong time; they got hurt because another person was projecting his or her own unhealed pain on them. This awareness can be a great burden lifted and allows the hurt person to see his or her hurt differently and to take it less personally. It can also develop some empathy, as the next question is, "Well, if it wasn't about me in the first place, then what was it about? What was inside the person who hurt me?" This is a step toward real understanding.

The second type of forgiveness tested is spiritually based twelve-step-oriented forgiveness used by Project MATCH in the United States. In this approach, addicts who have harmed others are encouraged to apologize for their wrongdoing, thereby making attempts at restitution. According to Hart, "Seeking forgiveness through the amends process requires incredible humility; the assistance of a Higher Power (God) helps people to transcend their ego, which normally balks when asked to admit mistakes." He goes on to say, "We think the two treatments can help people in addiction recovery drop the burden of carrying around pain from the past."

These two approaches to forgiveness—gaining empathy if we're the hurt party, and making amends if we're the offending party—are useful cornerstones in our own practical approach to forgiveness. Twelve-step work has long recognized the need for addicts or those who have perpetrated wrongs to do the Ninth Step: "Made amends to those we had hurt except when to do so would harm them or others."

Keeping spirituality and science separate was a notion that took root in the early seventeenth century but as we deepen our understanding of science and quantum physics, this theory is losing favor and giving way to a kind of thinking wherein one can be spiritual without necessarily identifying with a particular religion. Though we want to make therapy "scientific" any really good therapist knows that healing is also a matter of the heart and the heart cannot be measured, nor can character. Measuring the impact of prayer is a way to explore these questions, though that can be measured as we'll see in our next section. I grew up in the Greek Orthodox Church, which still embraces mysticism and this has made all forms of spirituality seem very beautiful, important, and undogmatic thanks to my very open-minded priest as a child, Father Anthony Coniaris. Even when I spent five years in my twenties as part of an ashram, studying Eastern philosophy and traveling to India, what he seemed most interested in was how it had affected me spiritually. Because he himself was such a spiritual man, he could tell it had only served to increase my understanding. I never felt that it conflicted with my Christian faith in any way, it only deepened it.

The mindfulness movement seems to me to be an organic one that allows us to drop down and go within, to deepen our connection with self and life.

The Power of Prayer

In 1986, Dr. Larry Dossey, a physician in Dallas, learned of a study that spoke to him and to what he had, to this point, been only a quiet witness of among his patients. Namely, that there was a clear relationship between one's mental states and their ability to heal. The study that came across his desk was both rigorous and scientific, its ethical design and startling results changed Dossey's life as a physician forever.

My resistance to using prayer in my medical practice was not unique. Almost all scientifically oriented physicians experience it. It simply is difficult to retain a spiritual instinct if one travels the path of science. The message of modern medical education is clear: one must choose either logical, analytical, and rational approaches, or irrational, religious, superstitious, and 'right-brained' ones, which include prayer. But the choice between science and spirituality appears increasingly artificial today, even from a scientific perspective. It is possible to tell a new story, one that allows science and spirituality to stand side by side in a complementary way, neither trying to usurp or eliminate the other. (Dossey)

For Dossey the results of these studies were too significant to be ignored. They showed that patients in a coronary care unit who were prayed for daily did better on average than patients who were not being prayed for. Simple? Intuitive even? But the design of the study was double blind, not only did the patients not know they were being prayed for, but those praying didn't know specifically who their prayers were aimed towards. Neither the nearly 400 patients nor their doctors and nurses knew who had been randomly assigned to the group being prayed for. Dr. Dossey was now motivated to search further. He uncovered more than 100 studies on the impact of prayer that he found to be rigorous and well-designed. More than half of the studies he read concluded that prayer positively affected everything from the healing of wounds and the reduction of high blood pressure to the behavior of fungi, yeast, leukemic white blood cells, cancer cells, tumors in mice, and germinating seeds in laboratory tests.

Dossey was well aware that the medical community would receive this news with skepticism. I remember years ago speaking at a conference with him and meeting him over lunch, a glowing man who sparkled when he spoke of the scientific power of prayer, I remember him saying something like "the research on the power of prayer to heal is so compelling that if the drug companies could bottle it, they'd be making millions if not billions." He openly shared his story. "I guess I run the risk of being disowned by practically all parties, the New Agers are not very happy with my stress on using science to guard against personal illusion, and the scientists don't want to talk about it (prayer)."

Ultimately, Dr. Dossey's aim is to prove the existence of a dimension of human reality that escapes the limits of the body, death, and time. In his book *Healing Words*, he writes that prayer "is the Universe's affirmation that we are immortal and eternal, that we are not alone." Sounding both like a physician and the minister he didn't become, Dr. Dossey says that "my real quarry" is "an antidote to the fear of death that has caused more misery in human history than all the diseases put together."

Dossey believes that this seemingly miraculous healing through prayer is most closely associated with a phenomenon known as "entanglement" from chaos theory. In quantum physics, entangled particles remain connected so that actions performed on one affect the other, even when separated by great distances. The phenomenon so riled Albert Einstein, he called it "spooky action at a distance."

Anyone who is in twelve-step programs will recognize this experience, "I am so bugged with _____, he/she is living rent free in my head."

"Try praying for them. I know it sounds like you won't want to do it, but it really does work." This is a common prescription in the rooms if you have someone in your life who you struggle with or even hate. What people in recovery have discovered intuitively is that something happens when you pray for someone, and that something that happens may be within the person being prayed for as well as the person praying. Somehow when we pray for someone, we are changing something not only for us but for them.

"Altruism behaves like a miracle drug," says Dossey in *Meaning & Medicine: A Doctor's Tales of Breakthrough and Healing,* "and a strange one at that. It has beneficial effects on the person doing the helping— the helper's high; it benefits the person to whom the help is directed; and it can stimulate healthy responses in persons at a distance who may view it only obliquely. Although studies on altruism and the helper's high sometimes employ the complex language of neurotransmitters, receptor sites, and chemicals such as endorphins, these behaviors are really not esoteric. We all know it feels good to *do something* nice for someone else and/or share a moment of good connection."

While no one can fully understand just *why* prayer works, study after study finds *that* it works. And it works based on laws of the universe. Why do waves work? Why does sunlight shine? How do cell phones connect? What's TV?

Certainly, it makes sense that aligning ourselves with what is happy, positive, prayerful, and awe-inspiring will take us on an invisible journey toward more of it. Tuning our emotional radio dial to happy somehow vibrates out into the ether and connects us with other similarly tuned waves.

Bruce Lipton says that if you think bad thoughts about someone, through this phenomenon of entanglement, they will think some about you. And he feels the opposite is true as well; thoughts and perhaps their accompanying emotions travel together. So healing is not only about identifying and feeling your feelings, it's about transforming them.

Opening up and sharing our innermost selves with a community of like-minded people and knowing that there is a worldwide network of people doing the same, changes us on the inside. And having the intention of healing and compassion, both for ourselves and others, changes us in our relationship to the world.

One of the most moving stories that I have heard on the power of program came from a psychodrama trainee who is Jewish and has strong ties to Israel. There was a twelve-step meeting where both Israelis and Palestinians were in attendance. As we say in the rooms, "it's a meeting" and if you need a meeting, that comes first, sobriety. So one-by-one those who came peeled off any identifying clothing or packs, put them away, and sat together. The meeting went on as meetings do, a speaker, sharing, listening. And at the end of the meeting, those there stood, joined hands and said the serenity prayer.

God, grant me the Serenity to accept the things I cannot change,
Courage to change the things I can.
And the Wisdom to know the difference.

— Reinhold Niebuhr
(adopted by all twelve-step programs)

Letter Writing

Write a letter to yourself, forgiving yourself for whatever you are holding against yourself.

Dear _____

_____

_____

_____

_____

_____

_____

_____

_____

_____

_____

_____

_____

_____

_____

_____

_____

_____

_____

Letter Writing

Write a letter of forgiveness to someone you are harboring anger and resentment toward.

Dear _____

_____

_____

_____

_____

_____

_____

_____

_____

_____

_____

_____

_____

_____

_____

_____

_____

_____

_____

_____

_____

_____

From, _____

Letter Writing

Write a letter that you would like to receive from someone else, forgiving you for something you imagine they are holding against you.

Dear _____

_____

_____

_____

_____

_____

_____

_____

_____

_____

_____

_____

_____

_____

_____

_____

_____

_____

_____

From, _____

Letter Writing

Write a letter that you would like to receive from someone else, asking you for your forgiveness of wrongs you feel were done to you.

Dear _____

_____

_____

_____

_____

_____

_____

_____

_____

_____

_____

_____

_____

_____

_____

_____

_____

_____

_____

_____

_____

_____

_____

_____

_____

From, _____

Letter Writing

Write a letter to God. Divide the paper into three. At the bottom, write the situation you are working with; and at the top, write the situation as you would like it to be. Leave the middle blank for spirit to work.

Dear _____

_____

_____

_____

_____

_____

_____

_____

_____

_____

_____

_____

_____

_____

_____

_____

_____

_____

_____

_____

_____

_____

_____

_____

From, _____

CHAPTER SIXTEEN

Resilience: Making Recovery Sustainable and Renewable

> When we tackle obstacles, we find hidden
> reserves of courage and resilience we did not know we had.
> And it is only when we are faced with failure, do we realize
> that these resources were always there within us.
> We only need to find them and move on with our lives."
>
> —A. P. J. Abdul Kalam

W hat goes into creating resilience is a question of increasing interest to researchers. Those who study it are finding that resilience encompasses innate qualities such as intelligence, ingenuity, and creativity that may be strengthened or even created through meeting and overcoming life challenges, *alongside* an ability to work with and mobilize available supports, to identify and make use of the help and resources that might be around. Rather than rejecting the support that is out there whether from a relative, friend, school or faith institution, a resilient child will likely find a way to embrace it and use it to get their lives to work. They will find a way to feel better rather than worse, to feel emboldened rather than helpless.

If you took the ACE Inventory on *tiandayton.com/soulfuljourney* and after that you took the Resilience Inventory, you may have found that those who can handle adverse experiences the most successfully, have high resilience scores. Even though their ACE score may be high and they've faced many adverse childhood experiences, they've found the kind of resilience to meet life challenges and still thrive and even grow from them.

But there is one cardinal finding that emerges in virtually all of the studies, including the longest one Emmy Werner conducted in Kauai, Hawaii. Resilient children have at least *"one consistent bonded relationship,"* one person who cares about them and by being a compassionate presence in their lives, helps the child to feel valued, to feel they are worth something. Resilience strengthens when there is someone in the child's life who is devoted, who communicates and guides. Successful communication loops between parent/caring person and child, and respectful interactions actually strengthen resilience. It makes sense, when children are helped to understand why it's good to work through the slings and arrows that inevitably come their way, when they are helped to understand how to cope and even grow from adversity, they develop a sense of mastery and self-respect. They can face challenges because they have the tools and they feel they are not alone. They feel valued enough to value themselves.

Emmy Werner also refers to the resilient child's ability to "attract mentors" and to make good use of those relationships. All of this speaks to the social context of resilience—successful kids don't get that way in isolation; they find and make use of others.

In the early days of resilience research, the focus was on 'the invulnerable child,' who did better than expected despite adversities and disadvantages...[D]evelopmental psychologists were interested in individual differences and the protective factors that contributed to the development of the invulnerable child. (Wong and Wong, 2012 p. 585)

But in more recent studies, we see the emphasis being placed on the resilient child's ability to mobilize supports. We can extrapolate that feeling valued and important to someone seems to allow kids to value themselves and having established a nourishing and satisfying connection teaches them how to trust and reach out.

"Resilience depends on supportive, responsive relationships and mastering a set of capabilities that can help us respond and adapt to adversity in healthy ways," says Jack Shonkoff, MD, director of the Center on the Developing Child at Harvard. "It's those capacities and relationships that can turn toxic stress into tolerable stress."

Here are some of the basic factors that appear over and over again as common threads when it comes to understanding what goes into creating resilience. Resilient kids tend to have:

- The availability of at least one stable, caring, and supportive relationship between a child and an adult caregiver.
- A sense of mastery over life circumstances.
- Strong executive function and self-regulation skills.
- The supportive context of affirming faith or cultural traditions. (Walsh, 2015)

Wong and Wong propose that certain qualities of behavioral resilience can only be developed from actual experience of having overcome adversities (Wong and Wong, 2012). I would argue that this is exactly what recovery is all about: you need to experience recovery in order to recover, "to get your soles in the (twelve-step) room," to accumulate days of attending meetings and doing recovery-oriented activities. It's not only about what you learn, it's about what you experience. As the

Chinese saying goes, "I hear and I forget, I see and I remember, I do and I understand." These researchers identified at least three typical patterns that resilient people appear to display that I think are useful to know. They see these qualities as being developed through facing and meeting life's challenges; they are dynamic, constantly evolving qualities rather than qualities residing only within the individual. In my experience, they also describe those who do well in recovery.

1. *Recovery:* bouncing back and returning to normal functioning.
2. *Invulnerability:* remaining relatively unscathed by the adversity or trauma in their lives in terms of their ability to function well.
3. *Post-traumatic growth:* bouncing back and becoming stronger, learning and growing through adversity. (Wong and Wong, 2012).

I believe in the "invulnerability" finding they are talking about basic easily quantified types of functioning such as work and self-support etc. I do not believe they are measuring their capacity for intimacy and relational connection. I think this finding may be limited in this way. Adult children can function as we know very well in certain areas of their lives, but their private relationships can suffer.

In their research on children from families affected by violence, poverty, substance abuse, racism, or family disruption, Sybil and Steven Wolin found that one of the qualities that resilient people often possessed was "survivor's pride" or a feeling of having met their challenges and prevailed. One can hear this in soldiers who have faced life-and-death situations and survived or from addicts who are sober and in good recovery or from ACAs who have figured out how to leave the dysfunction in their family behind and create happy lives of their own. Doing something on one's own behalf, mobilizing to make a situation better, rather than collapsing into helplessness is core to resilience.

Sybil and Steven Wolin (1994) looked at what personal qualities went into resilience in ACAs. They identified seven qualities that helped them to thrive where others did not.

- *Insight.* This is the ability to see people and situations in some degree of depth. They are able to see into a situation, they are perceptive and can benefit from their discerning awareness.
- *Independence.* Resilient kids and adults, Wolin and Wolin found, had a natural or perhaps a developed independence; they could think for themselves, act autonomously, and also create space between themselves and their troubles or difficult situations or families.
- *Relationships.* Resilient people were able to have and enjoy relationships and to feel sustained, supported, and nourished by them. They could give as well as accept caring from others.
- *Initiative.* This refers to the ability to take initiative on one's own or another's behalf, to take action to make a situation better, and to hang in there and show perseverance and doggedness.
- *Creativity.* Resilient kids and adults can come up with creative solutions to complex problems; they can think outside of the box. They also often have their own creative sides and can take pleasure and pride from their own creative endeavors or appreciate and enjoy those of others.
- *Humor.* Resilient people keep their sense of humor; they are able to turn a tough situation on its head and have a laugh at it.
- *Morality.* Resilient people tend to have a moral code that they live by, one from which they can draw strength and a sense of direction. It can relate to spirituality, to nature, to the universe, or to living a good and decent life for one's self and others.

Wolin and Wolin also found that ACAs who were doing well seemed to locate themselves at a "magic 200-mile radius" or more away from their families; they were able to get some distance that seemed to translate into emotional space.

Because we're wired by evolution to scan for danger, to identify threat in a split second, and gear up to self-protect we have a natural bias towards perceiving potential hazards. Psychologists refer to this very natural phenomenon as the "negativity bias." We need to be aware of this tendency to see threat so quickly and counter it with positive thinking.

Dr. David Perlmutter, neurologist, explains:

> We are given ideas that we think we need to live up to and as such never achieve a sense of total worth. Because the ideas that we feel we need to live up to are unachievable. When we look at people's selfies, they're always having the best time, they're singing and happy, when in reality we know that that isn't necessarily true. That there is adversity in everyone's life. I think that it's very important not to look at whether the glass is half full or half empty but to recognize moment to moment, that *the glass is absolutely overflowing.* We live in the best time ever for humanity, we live in a time when there is the least amount of war, we have resources that we've never had before. But into each life some rain must fall, we will all face adversity and that's part of the script. The question is, how do you deal with it when you recognize that adversity is to be expected, that our parents will die, that things can happen to our children, to ourselves? When we recognize and embrace that . . . we [see] it's all part of the play that is written for each and every one of us. . . . The question isn't only what happened, it's what do you choose to do with that event? I think it's reasonable to experience it to its upmost level of pain possible, but then let it go. Because it does not serve you to continue to machinate over this devastating experience, that each and every one of us will experience. (Perlmutter, 2019)

As a psychologist who has worked for decades with resilient people, I would say that invulnerability can be somewhat misunderstood. In my experience, people do not remain unscathed, nor do I think that would even be realistic or necessarily desirable. I find that even resilient people carry significant wounds from childhood that need to be addressed and take many years of therapy and twelve-step help to get past. But they see them differently, these are the people who have learned to embrace difficulties, to see them as challenges, to find the juice to transform pain into positivity through digging deep into themselves and coming up with strength, patience, and faith that they didn't know they had, which is part of their post-traumatic growth. They work daily toward appreciation and gratitude for the life they have, rather than bemoan what they don't have. And each day, that appreciation makes the life they have just a little bit brighter. They are recovery warriors who come to see those wounds as one of the most meaningful parts of their post-traumatic growth.

On this page, find a picture or pictures of yourself feeling great. Hopefully you have pictures from childhood on.

Paste the pictures on the page and then mentally reverse roles with yourself in each photo, at each age, and write a couple of sentences about how you're feeling at that moment, at that age.

E.g. I'm Maria and this is my new dress, I feel like I am a princess, today is my _____ birthday, etc.

_____

_____

_____

_____

_____

_____

_____

_____

_____

_____

_____

_____

_____

_____

_____

_____

On this page, find a picture or pictures of yourself as a child. Choose a
picture(s) that draws you for some
reason, one(s) in which you sense
that you have something to say...
Mentally reverse roles with yourself in that picture and say what
you need to say... Go....

_____

_____

_____

Now speak back to
yourself in that picture
from the age you are
now. Talk to that part
of you at that age
from today, tell that
part of you what
you need to hear.
Go....

_____

_____

_____

_____

_____

_____

_____

_____

A special thank you. On this page, put a picture or pictures of people (or pets) who you want to thank for being there for you. Looking at this picture, what feelings of gratitude come up? Write them down as if you were writing a thank you card. Thank you for…

_____

_____

_____

_____

_____

_____

_____

_____

_____

_____

This is your family photo page. Find pictures of your family of origin that pull you, for some reason, and put them here or another piece of paper. Now mentally reverse roles with every person in that picture and speak their inner life, what you imagine is going on inside of them that never really got said out loud. Do this for happy times, sad times, and so forth; do it as many times as you wish to. Go . . .

_____

_____

_____

_____

_____

_____

_____

_____

_____

_____

_____

_____

_____

_____

_____

_____

_____

_____

_____

_____

Now find a picture of yourself today in the life you have created, your family, friends, your partner, your children, grandchildren, pets, and so on. Write a sentence or two to each of them from your heart to theirs.

Tell each of them what they mean to you and what your wishes for them are.

On this page, put a picture of yourself today. Now write directly to yourself, telling yourself what your wishes, hopes, dreams and commitments are for your future. Describe the life you want to walk into beginning today and as far into your future as you want to visualize.

The Breakthrough Timeline

Instructions: At the appropriate year, write breakthrough moments when you made a good decision or got on the right track, moments when it all made sense.

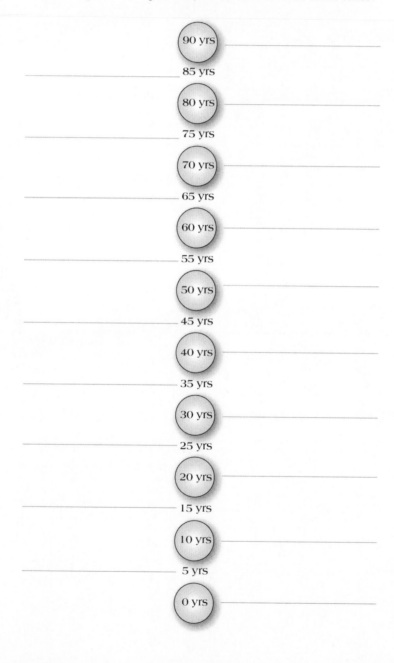

The Breakthrough Timeline

Answer the following questions:

1. What do you notice after doing this timeline?

_____

_____

_____

_____

2. What strengths do you feel you developed through facing and dealing with adversity in your life?

_____

_____

_____

_____

3. Was there a moment you look back on that surprises you in some way and if so why?

_____

_____

_____

_____

4. What compliment would you like to give yourself looking at your timeline?

_____

_____

_____

_____

5. Any person come to mind who really was there when you needed them? If so who and what do you want to say to them?

_____

_____

_____

_____

6. Are some periods of your life more filled with painful stuff than other times? Any surprises?

_____

_____

_____

_____

7. Do you notice a difference between your life and how you felt about yourself and your relationships before or after particularly painful or traumatic moments or periods? Describe the differences. Any new awarenesses about yourself or your life after doing this timeline?

_____

_____

_____

_____

CHAPTER SEVENTEEN

Emotional Sobriety and Emotional Literacy: Learning to Live in Balance

> It's dark because you are trying too hard.
> Lightly child, lightly. Learn to do everything lightly.
> Yes, feel lightly even though you're feeling deeply.
> Just lightly let things happen and lightly cope with them.
>
> —Aldous Huxley

E motional sobriety is a mind/body phenomenon. It encompasses the ability to experience and talk about feelings alongside learning to live life in balanced ways so that both the mind and the body can live in harmony. Bill W., the founder of Alcoholics Anonymous, coined the term. He saw sobriety from a substance as the addict's first task, the next challenge or "next horizon" he felt was emotional sobriety. And this is true for addicts and anyone who has lived with addiction or the emotional dysregulation that accompanies relational trauma. This is the point of this book, that relational trauma is dysregulating to our mind

Emotional Sobriety Graph

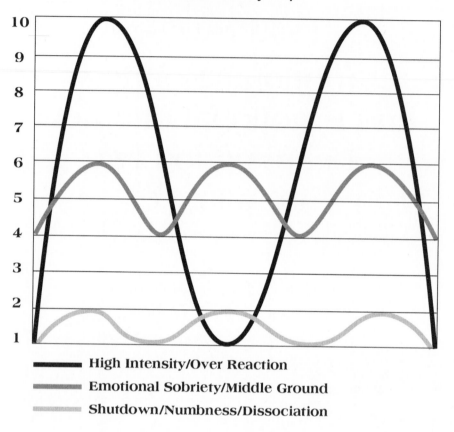

━━━━━ **High Intensity/Over Reaction**

━━━━━ **Emotional Sobriety/Middle Ground**

━━━━━ **Shutdown/Numbness/Dissociation**

and body and that it is up to us to restore our emotional balance. That we take ownership over ourselves and all that is in our personal sphere, that we get our own life to work and extend care and love to those lives that we touch and in this way, we influence the world. Lives change one by one, the world changes person by person, let it begin with *me*.

Emotional sobriety isn't about being overly serious; it's about not feeling, thinking, and behaving from emotional extremes. It's about self-regulation. We are less attached to our emotions, so to speak; we expand our ability to tolerate what we're feeling, gain information, and allow our feelings to inform us, we have them, feel them, think about, process and move through them. We can step back from them and perceive our own role in the play of life, in the scheme of things. We can see the big picture.

Learning the Language of Feelings

One of the stepping stones towards emotional sobriety is emotional literacy. Being able to translate our emotions into words elevates both feelings and limbic body memories from an unconscious state into a conscious one. This is what allows the thinking mind to come on board so that the beautiful prefrontal cortex can play it's function of creating meaning out of experience and placing it into the framework of our lives.

Emotional literacy constitutes nothing less than learning a new language, the language of feelings. When you become emotionally literate, your ability to translate feelings into words serves as a map that allows you to enter into your own inner world, travel through it and find your way out again. And then you can communicate that inner world to others. Simple as that sounds, it's not easy. It is a skill best developed in childhood, in the caring arms of our parents and caregivers who first and most importantly allow us to have an inner world of our own. Who listen as we struggle to find the right words, at the right time, for the right feeling, so that our fledgling attempts at being understood can actually be heard?

This language of emotions begins before words. Before language even enters the picture, we communicate our needs and wants to our parents and caregivers through an ever-expanding repertoire of looks, noises, screeches, facial expressions, gestures and body positions. An outreached hand, an arched back, a slap, a coo, a facial expression and a cuddle are the baby's way of expressing themselves and for the parent who cares, they are loaded with grammar, meaning and syntax.

Children have a language all their own, and it is up to the adults in their world to pay attention, so that they feel heard. So that they can know themselves and walk through the world as confident little beings who feel that they can be seen and understood for who they are. In the mind of a child, if our parents understand us, we carry an inner sense that the world will understand us. If our parents do not turn away from our fragile attempts to communicate what is going inside of us, then the world perhaps, will have time for us, too and we develop the inner strength to fight our way through to make ourselves understood if and when we feel ignored. When this process happens day-by-day throughout our childhood, with the people we love and want to be understood by the most, through our primary attachment figures, it will feel as if it comes naturally to us, and we will have a much better chance of understanding ourselves. If it doesn't, we will have to learn emotional literacy later in life.

That's both the bad and the good news. The bad news is that we have to learn it; the good news is that we can, and learning it later in life can be a soulful and exciting journey.

Finding the right words for the right feelings liberates our truth, and as Max Plank's quote from the beginning of the book said, "The truth is like a lion. You don't have to defend it. Let it loose. It will defend itself." Once we can use words to put shape and nuance into our inner experience, once we can communicate who we are on the inside, how we feel about something to ourselves and another human being, doors fly open. We can "know ourselves." This is one of the most empowering odysseys anyone can take in life: the journey within. This is what allows us to explore our inner world. To reflect on our feelings and create meaning and understanding. Only then can we become reflective about our emotions, ponder their meaning and significance within our self and our life, and share them with another person, then listen as another person does the same. Only then can we use the beauty of our thinking minds to bring balance and order to our inner world. Emotional literacy is part of how we create emotional sobriety and emotional intelligence. Both require that we feel our feelings and name them, that we become curious about our own inner experience and learn to hear ourselves.

And if we want intimacy, that we become curious about the inner experience of others.

Emotional Dyslexia

People who lack emotional literacy have a hard time identifying their feelings and naming them. It's as if they are emotionally color blind, they have trouble distinguishing between emotions or even seeing certain ones. Just as someone with dyslexia "sees" letters or words reversed or mixed up, people with what we might call emotional dyslexia, have trouble ordering feelings or perceiving emotional sequence. Feelings are jumbled together and indistinguishable from each other. They may misread their own emotions and the emotions of others.

A loss of emotional regulation, which manifests as a loss of emotional sobriety, has a pernicious and pervasive impact on our lives and our relationships. It can manifest as difficulty in regulating anxiety, depression, and moods, whether euphoric or depressive, or in a dysregulated relationship with food, alcohol, drugs, exercise, sex, shopping, work—you name it. This is one of the ways that pain gets passed down through the generations, through these types of chronic dysregulation.

Janet Woititz used to talk about how ACAs see living in 4, 5, and 6 as boring, we get used to "too much" or "too little"—we adapt to the see-saw, the roller coaster. But 4, 5, and 6 is underrated; it's actually that beautiful midrange that can allow us to live more fully in the present because we're not either peeling ourselves off the ceiling or trying to get up off the floor. We're not using all of our energy living in emotional extremes, which makes it available to use as we wish.

Living in 4, 5 and 6 means that we can use our emotions as information, feelings inform us rather than run us, and our thinking can then be clear. We can think coherently if we're not caught up in stereotyped, calcified reactions, if we're not spinning around in our heads.

Every part of the human response to trauma is about getting away from the here and now, blocking what's happening or fighting off the moment. Everything about healing from trauma is about coming back into the present, embracing the moment, and experiencing what we're feeling and sensing. As we come back into the here and now, we may feel the feelings, thoughts, and ideas that we ran from on our way out. And as we do that, we heal.

Recovery is preventative as well as curative. I see recovery for ACAs, codependents, and children of adverse childhood experiences as similar to the physical wellness movement. We not only work through the kinds of issues that block our ability to live happily, we build the strength, resilience and emotional intelligence that will make recovery and thriving sustainable and renewable. The wellness movement counters our crisis-oriented health culture in which we wait until our bodies have broken down and become sick to treat them. Recovery can do this for our emotional and mental health as we learn and adapt the kinds of lifestyles that actually help us to nourish and sustain mental, emotional, physical and spiritual well-being.

A constant focus on the past or a constant preoccupation with the future, knocks us out of where we want to be. Here. Continuously focusing on the painful parts of our past and re-litigating them over and over again, not only keeps us stuck in them, it creates more of them. We create new sets of feelings, new memories, and in this way get our present to mirror the most painful parts of our past. The idea is to not deny what hurt us, but to be able to feel it, think about it, and make new choices that we can live by. We cannot reach back in time and make what happened, un-happen. We cannot "un-ring the bell." But in the play of life, there is no need to, because the part of the past that is still alive in our present in a way that doesn't serve us will invariably make itself known and we can change *now, and now, and now.* And now. Because we're less preoccupied with the past or obsessing about the future, we're able to live more fully and mindfully in the present.

The here and now is our only real point of power. What we feel in the moment, see in the moment, and appreciate in the moment acts as a fertilizer for growing more of it. Attention is like watering the stuff of life; it grows more of whatever is watered.

I see the concepts surrounding recovery as important to generalize into the whole world these days. More than ever we need to strengthen our inner world in order to manage the increasing psychological and emotional demands placed on us through living in the global village of the cyber world. We could all use a twelve-step program or some self-help group that we can gain a sense of support and connection from. We need mindful living, slow eating, sober curiosity, green washing, nature prescriptions and relationships and these are the elements that are happening organically, Hi Tech-Hi Touch. We need ironically to come closer to ourselves in order to find the right distance or closeness from the rest of the world.

Twentieth-century psychologist Abraham Maslow, who is famous for his hierarchy of basic needs, believed in the power of what he called *the peak experience.* He believed the peak experience to be an essential component of identity that leads a person to feel whole, integrated, and in touch with themselves, others, and the mystery of life. It has always been my feeling that one of the reasons that the kinds of week-long experiential/psychodrama programs work so mysteriously well in jump-starting or accelerating personal growth and transformation is that they create a kind of peak experience. People gather purposefully in order to look within and they have help in doing just that. The best research on peak experiences has been done by Abraham Maslow who named and researched the phenomenon by studying people who have done things like climb Mount Everest, gone on spiritual quests, or engaged in the sorts of experiences that are in some way life altering. And I would add having a baby to that list; we are witnesses to and participants in life renewing itself, playing our part, feeling terrible pain but then forgetting it because we hold in our arms the promise and purpose of living. We become part of the mystery of life, the grand scheme of things, and we feel whole and integrated into the fabric of creation in a way that is impossible to put into words.

Maslow names the following qualities that people who have gone through peak experiences identify as being a part of their personal transformation. They also echo the qualities on *The Post Traumatic Inventory* as well; they are part of healing from trauma, part of the soulful journey of recovery. People who've undergone a peak experience, as well as, I believe, those who embrace the inner transformation that recovery offers, exhibit these qualities:

1. They are reality oriented.
2. They accept themselves, other people, and the natural world.
3. They have a great deal of spontaneity and aliveness.
4. They are problem solvers, rather than problem dwellers.
5. They have an air of detachment and a need for privacy.
6. They tend to be autonomous and independent.
7. Their appreciation of people and things is fresh rather than stereotyped.
8. Most of them have had profound mystical or spiritual experiences, although not necessarily religious in character.
9. They have a sense of empathy and altruism.
10. Their intimate relationships with a few specially loved people tend to be profound and deeply emotional rather than superficial.
11. Their values and attitudes are inclusive.
12. They do not confuse means with ends.
13. They have a sense of fun, and their sense of humor is philosophical rather than hostile.

14. They have a great fund of creativity.
15. They resist conformity to the culture.
16. They see the big picture and transcend the environment rather than just coping with it.

When you have been doing this work as long as I have and seen the miracles that happen for people and their lives and families, you can't help but have the deepest and most constant wish that all those who you know, and through my writing many of you who I have never met but somehow know, will embrace the miracle of recovery. And that you will allow the spirit of recovery to be at work in your life. As a psychologist and a psychodramatist, as a wife, mother, grandmother, daughter, aunt and sister, I have witnessed these personal transformations and breakthroughs over and over again. They appear to me to be born of deep desire, a lot of work in preparation, and then a kind of grace that manifests as moving past something, through something, and coming out on the other end, somehow feeling freer and more whole. As feeling simultaneously bigger but more right-sized. Colloquially, people have found ways to describe this phenomenon. Rebirth, an "aha," a come-to-Jesus moment, a personal transformation, a breakthrough or making a quantum leap. Whatever you call it, it's part of the mystery of life, of faith.

So if you will start walking, the path will appear beneath your feet. If you don't give up on life, life won't give up on you. You will no longer "regret, nor wish to close the door on your past" because it will become the doorway to becoming all that you can be, right now.

My advice to you, fellow traveler, is this:

Don't worry about making any one person the answer.

Let recovery be the answer.

Don't worry about finding that good mother.

Let the rooms embrace you.

Don't worry about the "God thing."

Let the "peace of the program grow inside you one day at a time."

Don't even worry about working the program.

Open yourself and let the program work in you.

Don't worry about finding yourself because if you walk this path, your Self will find *you*.

Don't worry about finding the path.

The path is inside of you, and you find it one step at a time.

Don't worry about finding a passion.

Let your passion lie in joyful and purposeful living.

Don't worry about the past because the past that you need to work through are those parts that interfere with your present.

They will show themselves to you if you are mindful and aware.

And, you will face them with courage, heart, and even joy.

Don't worry about the future because today well and mindfully lived,

Today loved and embraced,

Today faced and dealt with,

Are what you have, and they will shape your future.

Take it a day at a time.

Have faith.

Have heart.

Have courage.

Keep love in your heart.

You will be okay; you will be fine.

And more times than you think, your wildest dreams will come true.

Post Traumatic Growth Self-Test

Answer the following questions by placing a check (✔) in the box that best describes "where you are."

1. I changed my priorities about what is important in life.
   ❏ Almost none   ❏ Very little   ❏ Quite a bit   ❏ Very much

2. I have a greater appreciation for the value of my own life.
   ❏ Almost none   ❏ Very little   ❏ Quite a bit   ❏ Very much

3. I developed new interests.
   ❏ Almost none   ❏ Very little   ❏ Quite a bit   ❏ Very much

4. I have a greater feeling of self-reliance.
   ❏ Almost none   ❏ Very little   ❏ Quite a bit   ❏ Very much

5. I have a better understanding of spiritual matters.
   ❏ Almost none   ❏ Very little   ❏ Quite a bit   ❏ Very much

6. I more clearly see that I can count on people in times of trouble.
   ❏ Almost none   ❏ Very little   ❏ Quite a bit   ❏ Very much

7. I established a new path for my life.
   ❏ Almost none   ❏ Very little   ❏ Quite a bit   ❏ Very much

8. I have a greater sense of closeness with others.
   ❏ Almost none   ❏ Very little   ❏ Quite a bit   ❏ Very much

9. I am more willing to express my emotions.
   ❏ Almost none   ❏ Very little   ❏ Quite a bit   ❏ Very much

10. I know better that I can handle difficulties.
   ❏ Almost none   ❏ Very little   ❏ Quite a bit   ❏ Very much

11. I am able to do better things with my life.

  ❑ Almost none   ❑ Very little   ❑ Quite a bit   ❑ Very much

12. I am better able to accept the way things work out.

  ❑ Almost none   ❑ Very little   ❑ Quite a bit   ❑ Very much

13. I can better appreciate each day.

  ❑ Almost none   ❑ Very little   ❑ Quite a bit   ❑ Very much

14. New opportunities are available, which wouldn't have been otherwise.

  ❑ Almost none   ❑ Very little   ❑ Quite a bit   ❑ Very much

15. I have more compassion for others.

  ❑ Almost none   ❑ Very little   ❑ Quite a bit   ❑ Very much

16. I put more effort into my relationships.

  ❑ Almost none   ❑ Very little   ❑ Quite a bit   ❑ Very much

17. I am more likely to try to change things which need changing.

  ❑ Almost none   ❑ Very little   ❑ Quite a bit   ❑ Very much

18. I have a stronger spiritual faith.

  ❑ Almost none   ❑ Very little   ❑ Quite a bit   ❑ Very much

19. I discovered that I'm stronger than I thought I was.

  ❑ Almost none   ❑ Very little   ❑ Quite a bit   ❑ Very much

20. I learned a great deal about how wonderful people are.

  ❑ Almost none   ❑ Very little   ❑ Quite a bit   ❑ Very much

21. I better accept needing others.

  ❑ Almost none   ❑ Very little   ❑ Quite a bit   ❑ Very much

Reprinted with the permission of L. G. Calhoun and R. G. Tedeschi, can be contacted at: Department of Psychology—UNC Charlotte—Charlotte, NC 28223 USA.

How to Start Your Own
Peer Support Group

We seem to be living in a time where people want to go deeper, not to simply read but to have an experience for themselves. This is why I have designed this book with exercises, a website (*tiandayton.com /soulfuljourney*), and an action plan.

You can start a peer support group. If you choose to do this, here are some guidelines for safety and suggestions for formats:

I suggest that you meet once a month. More times get burdensome and fewer tend not to be enough to create momentum.

No Advice or Cross Talk

Have this as a ground rule; it's irresistible to give advice and to comment on what people are saying. Don't do either. This isn't therapy; it is a place to share and feel heard and supported—that's all. If people give advice, gently remind them of the ground rules. And obviously, no one makes money on this in any way.

Time Shares

I suggest you time your sharing, with three minutes being the outside time. If people go over, give them a "T" sign with your hands. Respecting time is important, so keep each other in line on this. Don't make it the responsibility of one person to manage time; it is everyone's responsibility.

Process

Read a chapter at home, and do the exercise. When you come to group you can either bring an exercise that you have all agreed to do at home, or you can do it together in your group. All groups are different; do what works for you and what you have time for.

Warm-Up

Start with an affirmation, open the book, I suggest *Forgiving and Moving On* or share an affirmation that you read over the week that is meaningful to you. Each person can share about what it brings up for them if you have time. If not, move to sharing about what doing a particular exercise brought up for you. I see no need for people to be in the same place in the book unless you want to do it that way. Personally I think it's fine for people to do the exercises during the month that they feel "warmed up" to or drawn to.

Sharing

Share about the experience of the exercise. This will likely be the bulk of your time together.

Closure

Listen to a guided imagery from *tiandayton.com* if that works for your group; decide together.

Some things you can add for fun depending on your group:

- Treats and/or a meal (each person can bring something or you can revolve hosting).
- Coloring Books: I have made coloring books with affirmations, you can begin or end a group with coloring. You can read affirmations and share about them as you color if you use them as people are arriving. You can make the entire group about coloring, sharing and visiting together if you want to keep it really simple. Coloring is social; it's fun and an easy way to relate to each other.

Coloring books and affirmation books are available wherever books are sold. To see some of my recommendations, visit *tiandayton.com*.

Sign up for the newsletter to receive two blogs/month and be alerted of my trainings.

REFERENCES

Alexander, Bruce K. *The Globalization of Addiction: A Study in Poverty of the Spirit.* New York: Oxford University Press, 2008.

Robert F. Anda, Vincent J. Felitti, David Brown, Daniel Chapman, Maxia Dong, Shanta R. Dube, Valeria Edwards, and Wayne Giles. "Insights into Intimate Partner Violence from the Adverse Childhood Experiences (ACE) Study." In *The Physician's Guide to Intimate Partner Violence and Abuse,* 77–88. 2nd ed. Volcano, CA: Volcano Press, 2006.

Anda, Robert F., Vincent J. Felitti, J. Douglas Bremner, John D. Walker, Charles Whitfield, Bruce D. Perry, Shanta R. Dube, and Wayne H. Giles. "The Enduring Effects of Abuse and Related Adverse Experiences in Childhood." *European Archives of Psychiatry and Clinical Neuroscience256,* no. 3 (2005): 174–86.

Anda, Robert F., MD, MS, and Vincent J. Felitti, MD. "ACE Reporter: Origins and Essence of the Study." (2003). http://thecrimereport.s3.amazonaws.com/2/94/9/3076/acestudy.pdf.

Bailey, Regina. "Amygdala's Location and Function." Thought Co. (2019). Accessed July 18, 2019. https://www.thoughtco.com/amygdala-anatomy-373211.

Carpi, John. "Stress: It's Worse Than You Think." *Psychology Today* (1996). Accessed July 25, 2016. https://www.psychologytoday.com/us/articles/199601/stress-its-worse-you-think.

Damasio, Antonio R. *Looking for Spinoza: Joy, Sorrow, and the Feeling Brain.* 1st ed. London: William Heinemann, 2003.

Dayton, Tian. *Emotional Sobriety: From Relationship Trauma to Resilience and Balance.* 1st ed. Deerfield Beach, FL: Health Communications, 2007.

Dispenza, Joe. *Breaking the Habit of Being Yourself: How to Lose Your Mind and Create a New One.* 4th ed. Carlsbad, CA: Hay House, 2013.

Dispenza, Joe, Dr. *You Are the Placebo: Making Your Mind Matter.* Carlsbad, CA: Hay House, 2014.

Dong, Maxia, Robert F. Anda, Vincent J. Felitti, Shanta R. Dube, David F. Williamson, Theodore J. Thompson, Clifton M. Loo, and Wayne H. Giles. "The Interrelatedness of Multiple Forms of Childhood Abuse, Neglect, and Household Dysfunction." *Child Abuse & Neglect* 28, no. 7 (2004): 771-84. doi:10.1016/j.chiabu.2004.01.008.

Dossey, Larry, MD. Meaning & Medicine: Lessons from a Doctor's Tales of Breakthrough and Healing. New York: Bantam, 1992.

Dyer, Trey. "Cross Addiction," DrugRehab.com., 2019.

Felitti, Vincent J., Robert F. Anda, Dale Nordenberg, David F. Williamson, Alison M. Spitz, Valerie Edwards, Mary P. Koss, and James S. Marks. "Relationship of Childhood Abuse and Household Dysfunction to Many of the Leading Causes of Death in Adults: The Adverse Childhood Experiences (ACE) Study." *American Journal of Preventive Medicine* 14, no. 4 (1998): 245-58.

Grant, Jon E., Marc N. Potenza, Aviv Weinstein, and David A. Gorelick. "Introduction to Behavioral Addictions." *The American Journal of Drug and Alcohol Abuse* 36, no. 5 (2010): 233-41.

Hagedorn, W. Bryce. "The Call for a New Diagnostic and Statistical Manual of Mental Disorders Diagnosis: Addictive Disorders." *Journal of Addictions & Offender Counseling* 29, no. 2 (2009): 110-27.

Hart, Kenneth E., PhD. "A Spiritual Interpretation of the 12-Steps of Alcoholics Anonymous: From Resentment to Forgiveness to Love." *Journal of Ministry in Addiction & Recovery* 6, no. 2 (1999): 25-39.

Harris, Nadine Burke, MD. *The Deepest Well: Healing the Long-Term Effects of Childhood Adversity*. New York: Mariner Books, 2019.

Herman, Judith. Trauma and Recovery: The Aftermath of Violence—From Domestic Abuse to Political Terror. New York: Basic Books, 1997.

Injury Prevention and Control: Division of Violence Prevention. (2014, May 13). Retrieved from http://www.cdc.gov/violenceprevention/acestudy.

Ireland, Tom. "What Does Mindfulness Meditation Do to Your Brain?" *Scientific American*, 2014.

Levine, Peter A. *In an Unspoken Voice: How the Body Releases Trauma and Restores Goodness*. Berkeley, CA: North Atlantic Books, 2010.

Levy, Michael S. PhD. "A Helpful Way to Conceptualize and Understand Reenactments." *The Journal of Psychotherapy Practice and Research* 7 (3) (1998): 227–235.

Lipton, Bruce H. *The Biology of Belief: Unleashing the Power of Consciousness, Matter & Miracles*. Hay House, 2016.